Contents

Foreword

The current law relating to equal opportunities – particularly in the context of social work, education and training – is to be found in a number of diverse Acts of Parliament and decisions of the Courts. Surprisingly, there is no single guide to this subject despite a long standing demand from providers of social work and social care, education and training as well as CCETSW personnel. In this admirable handbook, Professor Preston-Shoot has addressed this important demand. He has provided a much needed guide to an understanding of the judicial basis for the practice of equal opportunities and the application of the law to social work education and training. His guide clarifies the nature of equal opportunities legislation in the United Kingdom and provides for an effective implementation of CCETSW's equal opportunities requirements.

CCETSW under the Health and Social Services and Social Security Adjudications Act 1983 is a statutory body, responsible for the development and promotion of education, training and qualifications for social work and social care staff in the statutory, voluntary and private sectors of the personal social services throughout the UK. Since 1989, CCETSW has required that those receiving training in the awards it gives should be equipped to work with all groups of people, many of whom experience various forms of disadvantage and discrimination. CCETSW has exercised this responsibility in accordance with the duties laid down in legislation covering the UK. Various sections in social care and social work have sought CCETSW's advice on the acceptable parameters of legitimate practice when the legislation and codes of practice have been unclear. CCETSW is keen to ensure that its providers and centres appreciate the full significance of its equal opportunities requirements in the context of equal opportunities legislation.

The publication of this book is therefore an important event for everyone concerned with understanding equal opportunities legislation and its application to social work and social care education, training and assessment. In addition to the excellent work of Professor Preston-Shoot acknowledgement is due to the able direction of CCETSW's Equal Opportunities Consultative Group members, and in particular Don Naik and Gill Michaels, who steered the tender specification, along with CCETSW staff, Liz Wulff-Cochrane and Naina Patel. The valuable comments by the Commission of Racial Equality, the Equal Opportunities

Commission and Rachel Dineley at Beachcroft Stanleys Solicitors on an earlier draft of the book are appreciated.

Jeffrey Greenwood
Chairman, CCETSW

Preface

Equal opportunities legislation, together with associated guidance and codes of practice, may set the parameters for lawful practice but the operational implications have not always been clear to providers of education and training. This guide was commissioned by CCETSW in order to assist providers to appreciate their statutory duties, and the legislative context to CCETSW's equal opportunities requirements. It therefore covers legislation relevant to social work and social care education, training and assessment.

Policy and practice across agencies increasingly emphasise partnership and involvement of stakeholders in all aspects of service planning, delivery and monitoring. With regard to equal opportunities policies, this commitment to involvement and partnership is gradually being reflected in research and project work. Variously known as partnership or emancipatory research (Everitt *et al.* 1992; Whitaker and Archer 1994), involving stakeholders promotes values of reciprocity, empowerment and partnership which are increasingly central to policy development. It enables stakeholders to participate in defining the issues to be understood, and in acquiring and analysing data. It ensures that research and project work address the questions which they regard as relevant, thereby avoiding the imposition of preconceptions.

This was the approach adopted in this guide which was commissioned to:
● address areas of uncertainty for providers;
● provide advice which they would find useful;
● illustrate how the law can be used to eliminate discrimination across the spectrum of social work and social care education and training; and
● identify good practice.

A number of consultation workshops and focus group meetings were held in all the nations of the United Kingdom, with people involved in National and Scottish Vocational Qualifications, the Diploma in Social Work and Post Qualifying provision and assessment. The purpose was to gather in one place information on issues, areas of uncertainty and problems faced by providers, together with examples of good practice. Questionnaires were also completed by some DipSW programme providers and NVQ assessment centre personnel who could not attend the workshops. Upwards of 100 people have been involved in generating ideas for the guide.

Structure of the guide

The major purpose of this guide is to clarify statutory duties which exist and to illustrate their application to the practice of social work and social care education and training. Accordingly, while anti-discriminatory and equal opportunities legislation is critically analysed where appropriate, readers looking for further such material will hopefully find the suggested further reading useful.

The guide is divided into four parts with a scene setting introduction. Part 1 explains the relationship between law, guidance and practice. Together with pointers from administrative law, it provides the framework for practice. Part 2 introduces the main pieces of anti-discriminatory and equal opportunities legislation, both their general provisions and those specific to education and training. These provisions are then applied in Part 3 to specific areas of education and training activity where readers may be looking for guidance. Part 4 draws out the implications for programme providers and offers suggestions for further reading. An index for use in conjunction with the contents is provided.

I hope that the book will prove useful and valuable to all those involved in social work and social care education and training. I have felt very encouraged by everyone's positive response to the project which has resulted in this guide. But before you read it please answer the questions on equal opportunities which follow this preface.

Michael Preston-Shoot
Liverpool John Moores University
July 1997

Questions on equal opportunities for programme providers

Consider the following questions, writing down your answers and the reasons for them. Then read the first 10 chapters before returning to these questions and reviewing your answers. If you revise your answers at that point, write down your reasons for so doing. Then read the remainder of the guide before returning again to these questions. What are your answers at this point, and why? Then consider how your answers are different from those you gave originally, and their implications for your working practices.

1   What do you understand by the term positive action?

2   What is the status of codes of practice issued by the Commission for Racial Equality and the Equal Opportunities Commission?

3   What differences are there between the Race Relations Act 1976, the Sex Discrimination Act 1975, and the Disability Discrimination Act 1995 in relation to:
    a types of discrimination prohibited?
    b positive action?
    c requirements placed on providers of education and training?

4   Are quotas lawful when seeking to enrol onto a programme:
    a black students?
    b women students?
    c disabled students?

5   What action would you take if there are two students, one black and one white, competing for the one remaining place, who had performed equally well at interview?

6   What action would you take when a student who has dyslexia does not want to submit assignments in writing?

7   What action should you and the placement agency take when a disabled student experiences difficulties, as a result of the disability, on placement?

8   What advice would you give a student who complains that another student has made offensive racial and sexual remarks to them?

9   What action would be appropriate when a student fails to

disclose a criminal conviction and this is revealed by a police check?

10 What requirements, derived from equal opportunities legislation, apply to academic institutions and agencies offering placements when:
   a recruiting students to courses?
   b assessing students?
   c considering their policy response to legislation?

11 What legislation applies in relation to language and the provision of education and training?

12 How is sexual harassment defined?

13 How is disability defined in law?

14 What differences exist in the applicability of equal opportunities legislation between the different nations within the United Kingdom?

15 Is discrimination on grounds of age and of sexuality lawful?

Acknowledgements

I am grateful to everyone who participated in the workshops and who completed questionnaires. This helped me to define the issues to be understood and the questions to be addressed in this guide. I am especially grateful to all those who provided me with information and references, who assisted in the organisation of the workshops, and who commented on drafts. I would particularly like to mention Kathryn Cameron (University of Strathclyde), Elaine Davies (CCETSW, Wales) and Patricia Higgins (CCETSW, Northern Ireland) who provided me with helpful guidance relating to the law in their countries.

The final version of the guide benefited greatly from the comments offered by Barbara Cohen (Commission for Racial Equality), Kamlesh Bahl (Equal Opportunities Commission) and Rachel Dineley (Beachcroft Stanleys Solicitors). I very much appreciate their support for this project.

I have also very much appreciated the support, guidance and advice of Naina Patel, Equal Opportunities Project Manager at CCETSW.

Michael Preston-Shoot
Liverpool John Moores University
July 1997

Abbreviations

AASW	Advanced Award in Social Work
CRE	Commission for Racial Equality
DDA	Disability Discrimination Act
DipSW	Diploma in Social Work
DEG	Department of Employment Group
DH	Department of Health
EOC	Equal Opportunities Commission
FEC	Fair Employment Commission
FE(NI)A	Fair Employment (Northern Ireland) Act
NDC	National Disability Council
NVQ	National Vocational Qualification
PQSW	Post Qualifying Award in Social Work
RADAR	Royal Association for Disability and Rehabilitation
RRA	Race Relations Act
SDA	Sex Discrimination Act
SSI	Social Services Inspectorate
SVQ	Scottish Vocational Qualification
WLA	Welsh Language Act 1993

Table of cases

Key

All ER	All England Law Reports
CA	Court of Appeal
CO	Crown Office
IRLR	Industrial Relations Law Reports
IT	Industrial Tribunal
WLR	Weekly Law Reports

Cases

Bracebridge Engineering Company v. Darby [1990] IRLR 3

Burton and Rhule v. De Vere Hotels [1996] IRLR 596

Commission for Racial Equality v. Fearn and British Electrical Repairs Ltd. [1987] Westminster County Court 8617528

Commission for Racial Equality v. Roper [1987] Unreported

De Souza v. Automobile Association [1986] IRLR 103

Hampson v. Department of Education and Science [1989] CA. IRLR 69

Jeffers v. North Wales Probation Committee [1995] IT 61385/93

Jones v. University of Manchester [1993] IRLR 218

Lambeth London Borough Council v. Commission for Racial Equality [1990] IRLR 231

Mandla v. Dowell Lee [1983] IRLR 209

McKenzie v. McKenzie [1970] 3 WLR 472

Ojutiku and Oburoni v. Manpower Services Commission [1982] IRLR 418

P. v. S. and Cornwall County Council [1996] IRLR 347

Padison v. IMI Cornelius (UK) Ltd. [1992] IT 9810/92

Porcelli v. Strathclyde Regional Council [1986] IRLR 134

R. v. Devon County Council, ex parte Baker and Johns [1995] CA. 1 All ER 72

R. v. Durham County Council, ex parte Curtis and Broxson [1995] CA. 1 All ER 72

R. v. Gloucestershire County Council and Another, ex parte Barry [1997] House of Lords. 2 All ER 1

R. v. Islington LBC, ex parte Rixon [1996] The Times 17 April

R. v. North Yorkshire County Council, ex parte Hargreaves [1994] CO/878/94

Circulars

EL(95)143 *Employing Disabled People in the NHS: A Guide to Good Practice* Leeds: NHS Management Executive
EL(96)4 *Ethnic Minority Staff in the NHS – A Programme of Action* Leeds: NHS Management Executive
LAC(93)12 *Further and Higher Education Act 1992: Implications for Sections 5 and 6 of the Disabled Persons (Services, Consultation and Representation) Act 1986* London: Department of Health
LAC(93)17 *Protection of Children: Disclosure of Criminal Background of those with Access to Children* London: Department of Health

Chapter 1
Introduction – Setting the scene

This guide is intended to clarify the law on equal opportunities and anti-discriminatory practice in the provision of social work education and training across the continuum of CCETSW awards. It will, additionally, explain the distinctions between the law, guidance and codes of practice, and will offer some signposts towards good practice. The suggestions, drawn from practice, are not offered as prescriptions but rather as possible ways of counteracting discrimination and promoting equal opportunities in provision. Not uncommonly, people look to the law for protection and direction, only to find that it does not always provide effective remedies, answers or, indeed, a coherent, unambiguous and consistent framework. The law is sometimes complex and problematic to apply. Whilst alone it is not an answer or remedy for discrimination, it provides one framework within which practice can be reasoned, debated and challenged.

The guide addresses issues and problems arising when providers of education and training confront discrimination and seek to implement equal opportunities. As such, the guide is a product of CCETSW's commitment to eliminating discrimination and disadvantage in education and training provision, and its responsibility to ensure that its equal opportunity policy is effectively implemented.

Several concerns point to the need for guidance.

First, social work academics and practice teachers may be uncertain about what parts of the law and associated guidance are mandatory. For instance, what does positive action mean in recruitment and selection for training? Some practitioners and agencies are struggling with defining and implementing anti-discriminatory practice, both generally and in relation to training (Balen *et al.* 1993; Smyth and Campbell 1996). Nor does training for practice teachers necessarily include inputs on the law relating either to social work practice or to discrimination, even though before being accredited their ability to plan learning opportunities for students to practise within the legal framework should be tested (Ball *et al.* 1995). That CCETSW has issued advice on legal matters and on issues arising from the recruitment of disabled students (Skidmore 1993; 1995) is an indication of practice uncertainty.

Secondly, evidence continues to accumulate of inequality and discrimination in education and training provision. A picture has emerged (de Gale 1991; de Souza 1991; Pink 1991) of discrimination in:

- *recruitment and selection* – with different levels of experience and/or qualifications required of black students, and unfair treatment in interviews;
- *assessment* – with an absence of marking criteria or inconsistent application of criteria and marking arrangements;
- *curricula structures* – using black students as race experts, or non-recognition of differences; neither course material nor the syllabus integrating anti-discriminatory practice and black perspectives;
- *staff attitudes.*

Thus, Coulson (1993) found that the students least likely to succeed were women, disproportionately black women from Asian and Afro-Caribbean communities. She identified individual, group and institutional racism in the teaching process and curriculum, in assessment, and in practice opportunities. Black students were more likely to have repeat or extended placements. Burgess *et al.* (1992) reported racism on training courses and conveyed the anger, frustration and disappointments which can result. They argued that institutions had failed to recognise their responsibility for black students and that, in not recognising their needs as different, institutions were failing to provide an equal chance to succeed. Bond (1996) identified how black staff may depend on supportive managers for positive experiences. Training may be available but does not always result in a formal qualification. Some training is inaccessible, causing frustration. Black staff need support to counter poor access to training before joining a social services department. Equally, providers of education and training need to consider how black students' positive experiences may be heard, and how the complex psychological and structural factors that affect black students' training in predominantly white organisations can be managed in a way that empowers them (Aymer and Bryan 1996).

Similar findings are reported about the experiences of disabled students, with evidence of collusion at recruitment and selection, inadequate assessment of a disabled student's special needs, and insufficient preparation to support disabled students on placement and in the academic curriculum. RADAR (1994), in identifying disappointing figures on the participation of disabled students in full-time further and higher education, has called for equality of opportunity in their academic, social and personal development. RADAR is particularly critical of lack of access, lack of appropriate

support structures, and the absence of mandatory funding for students whose disabilities oblige them to study part-time.

I:6 Evaluating their experiences of recruiting visually disabled students, James and Thomas (1996) found that discriminatory practices were seriously inhibiting the students' progress both before and during a DipSW course. Some agencies assumed that visually disabled students were unsuitable for most social work tasks. Similarly, Taylor (1996), researching the experiences of deaf students in social work and youth and community work training, found ad hoc and uncoordinated provision, ignorance of support needs and a poor level of resources. He pointed out that, given social work's value base, education and training should be the ideal place for students who experience oppression to study with a reasonable expectation of equal treatment. However, the barriers which students encountered had a detrimental effect on their study, on their ability to operate in their chosen occupation, and on their confidence and attainment levels.

I:7 For students from gay and lesbian communities, the picture is no better. Campbell (1995) reported negative attitudes among placement agency staff, while Logan and Kershaw (1994) and Trotter and Gilchrist (1996) provided evidence of heterosexism in organisations and the effect this may have on teachers and students alike.

I:8 In Northern Ireland, according to Smyth and Campbell (1996), organisations are often powerful sites of resistance to change and, in relation to counteracting sectarianism, agency policies are at best non-discriminatory and at worst compatible with the reproduction of sectarian divisions.

I:9 Thirdly, anti-discriminatory practice is good practice. This proposition partly rests on ethical grounds, namely that a failure to meet a person's needs, and to advocate for a person's well-being and the alleviation of disadvantage, is an act of injustice, an abuse of power. The proposition also rests on grounds of good management of people and resources as indicated in circular EL(95)143, namely that staff are used effectively and their valuable skills are retained and developed. Otherwise, the economic costs of low morale, grievances, and staff turnover quickly become apparent. Finally, the proposition draws support from notions of service efficiency and effectiveness. Organisations serve, interact with, and should provide a satisfactory and appropriate service for all sectors of the community. Accordingly, policies to counteract discrimination and promote equal opportunities should feature centrally in social work in order to ensure that services are appropriate and accessible to all communities.

However, what does it mean to organise education and training in accordance with the principles of equal opportunity? How might or should providers give real meaning to anti-discriminatory policies? What is an appropriate service and how should it be offered? If the challenge is to provide equal access, equal shares, equal treatment and equal outcomes (Young and Connelly 1984), how might such genuine equality be secured? It will prove difficult to monitor the effectiveness of any equal opportunity policy without some initial answers.

Finally, it is still possible to encounter denial of the requirement and importance for policies and practice guidelines to take account of people's differing needs, and to meet concerns about the resources required for delivering equal opportunities. The law provides a mandate for anti-discriminatory education and training provision in relation to race (now being extended to include Northern Ireland); gender; disability and, additionally, to religion in Northern Ireland and to language in Wales. Accordingly, training structures need to incorporate legal requirements and see anti-discrimination not as a problem or costly burden but as a fact (CCETSW 1994) to be reflected in relevant, high quality services. Integrating equal opportunity requirements into programme structures is cost effective.

The question then becomes how policies can best be implemented. Three concerns commonly arise here. First, allegiance to a formal policy which gives the appearance of organisational commitment often fails to translate into actual progress. Secondly, commitment may be to a short agenda, with a goal of equality of opportunity, rather than to a long agenda with goals of transformational change in organisations and of equality of outcomes (Cockburn 1991). A policy which merely opens doors will prove relatively ineffective if other circumstances prevent previously excluded people from accessing new opportunities. Equally, a policy can become a device to maintain underlying patterns of relationships, to retain rather than change the system as a system. Thirdly, the law has weaknesses and its scope is limited. Legislation and policies alone will not guarantee an end to discriminatory practices. Effectiveness and change also depend on education and training, on the breadth of the policy and the ease with which any procedures it creates can be used, and on monitoring and enforcement.

One key condition of progress is for change to be led by senior managers who champion equal opportunities (Cockburn 1991; Taylor 1992). A second is for policy to be constructed as a change strategy based on a full assessment of the current position, which commits staff and financial resources to implementation and includes an action plan with timetables, targets and review mechanisms to measure achievement. Assessment of progress must be built in, indicating for example where change and training are required. Sufficient power, support and authority should be provided to those responsible for the action plan to overcome resistance and to see through change. A third key condition of progress is to extend the meaning of equality. Not only must access into an organisation be promoted, but the type of organisation itself and the values and practices by which it wishes to be known and judged should be discussed.

Action plan for managers

The Commission for Racial Equality (CRE) and the Equal Opportunities Commission (EOC) in a manual for managers (1995) encouraged managers of further and higher education institutions to:
● build equal opportunities into strategic plans;
● give a high profile to equal opportunity commitments, distribute the policy widely, and take action to ensure staff understanding of equal opportunities issues and awareness of the legal framework, for example through training;
● allocate responsibility clearly for implementing the policy;
● conduct research to establish staff and student understanding of the policy, and awareness of their rights and responsibilities;
● communicate regularly with staff, students, relevant organisations concerned with equal opportunities, and local communities, and integrate their perspectives of the effectiveness of the policy into

review and report mechanisms;
- monitor the policy, with results capable of analysis by ethnic group and gender, and take action to remedy shortfalls.

Outstanding issues

Nonetheless, questions and areas of uncertainty remain. Among those encountered in preparatory research for this guide were the following:

- what is lawful in terms of recruitment and selection? What is the meaning of positive action? How can we encourage people to apply and meet targets for the numbers of black and disabled students?
- what guidelines might there be for selection of disabled and minority group students?
- what action should programmes take when few students are recruited from minority groups and/or when there are higher failure and drop-out rates for black students?
- what is an appropriate composition for an interview panel?
- what is good practice in relation to criminal convictions?
- access to buildings, and facilities (such as loop systems) for disabled students are limited. Staff do not always prepare material sufficiently ahead of time to facilitate translation into other languages or media;
- placement agencies vary in their responses to disabled students, and to anti-discriminatory practice. How should programmes respond to instances where employers are reluctant to employ or to open up training to people from particular groups?
- how can assessment be enabling rather than oppressive? How can programmes maintain standards, and ensure that assessment tasks are responsive to the needs of students and value their experiences and strengths?
- what counts as valid evidence for assessment, for instance in relation to language?

The purpose of this guide is to attempt some answers, to indicate the parameters of lawful practice.

Part I

The framework for practice

ACEGENDERLANGUAGE
ISABILITYEQUALOPPOR
UNITIESSEXUALITYLAW
UIDANCEPRACTICERACE
ENDERLANGUAGEDISA
LITYEQUALOPPORTUN
ESSEXUALITYLAWGUID

Chapter 2
The relationship between law and guidance

To understand the legal framework for practice, it is necessary to distinguish between Acts, regulations, guidance and codes of practice. Social welfare law, including the law relating to discrimination, rather than explicitly conferring rights on individuals, is usually expressed through powers and duties, responsibilities and prohibitions, which determine how organisations must or may act. Regulations, guidance and codes of practice connect these statutory duties and powers to principles for practice. They clarify how legislation is to be understood and implemented.

Regulations are drafted by civil servants to realise the intention of particular legislation, issued by the Minister under the relevant Act of Parliament, and have the full force of law. Government circulars and policy guidance on particular legislation, when issued under section 7 of the Local Authority Social Services Act 1970 (applicable to England and Wales only) have the same status as regulations and may be quoted in complaints procedures and court proceedings. Local authorities have been subject to judicial review for failing to implement section 7 guidance (for example, R v North Yorkshire County Council, ex parte Hargreaves [1994]). If such guidance is to be departed from, it must be with good reason, articulated in the course of some identifiable decision-making process, and the procedure adopted should not be substantially different (R v Islington London Borough Council, ex parte Rixon [1996]). Other guidance and circulars are intended to promote rather than to legislate for good practice, as are codes of practice. These, too, may be quoted in proceedings and regard must be had to them when authorities are carrying out their functions.

The Race Relations Act 1976 (RRA), Sex Discrimination Act (1975) (SDA), and Disability Discrimination Act 1995 (DDA) are among those Acts which may establish organisations and permit them to issue codes of practice. When these are approved by the responsible Government Minister, as in the case of the codes of practice concerning employment issued by the Commission for Racial Equality (CRE), the Equal Opportunities Commission (EOC) and, forthcoming, the National Disability Council (NDC), it is not an offence to disregard their provisions, nor does ignoring their provisions of itself create an act of discrimination, but their provisions may be taken into account in any proceedings (Malone 1993; Gooding 1996). Whether a code of practice has been followed is relevant to determining if a dismissal was fair (Padison v IMI

Cornelius (UK) *Ltd* [1992]). Industrial tribunals and courts may accept that small organisations will only require simpler procedures whereas more complex organisations will be expected to carry out all the detailed recommendations in these codes of practice. Other codes of practice are non-statutory and, therefore, stand as statements of good practice, to which it is expected organisations will pay due regard when performing their functions.

The SDA 1975; RRA 1976 and DDA 1995 do not require organisations to adopt equal opportunity policies. However, employers can be held responsible for the discriminatory acts of their employees, even if these acts have not been authorised or have been explicitly prohibited, unless they have taken all reasonable and practicable steps to prevent acts of discrimination (Malone 1993). Without an equal opportunity policy, which should include all the statutory requirements but may be broadened out to include other matters, it will be difficult for employers to establish that they have taken such steps and that employees have been made aware of what the law and their employers require of them.

CCETSW's authority to promote training

CCETSW derives its authority to promote training in social work from the Health and Social Services and Social Security Adjudications Act 1983. Under this Act, CCETSW has issued mandatory rules, which have been approved by the Privy Council, governing the provision of education and training leading to the DipSW. Otherwise, the documents which set out CCETSW's normal requirements may be quoted in complaints procedures and other proceedings, such as appeals against assessment decisions. Such documents cannot override the lawful policies of other agencies.

This is the legislative and regulatory context for CCETSW's own equal opportunities policy statement which applies to programme providers, students and candidates, and CCETSW employees. The full text may be found in the rules and requirements for the DipSW (CCETSW 1996). The policy statement is integrated into the requirements for qualification, particularly through the six DipSW values requirements and, in relation to NVQ, Unit 0. Overall, as the elements of this unit make clear, the onus is on people to recognise and understand the need for anti-discriminatory practice; to recognise and tackle different forms of discrimination; to understand and promote people's rights, strengths and uniqueness; and to promote appropriate services.

The European dimension

Finally, there is a European Union dimension on gender derived from Article 119 of the Treaty of Rome and five directives relating to equality of treatment between women and men. These measures include access to employment, vocational training, and promotion and working conditions. The directives lay down objectives which must be met by legislation in member states. The Equal Pay directive, for example, which established the principle of equal pay for work of the same or equal value, required an amendment (enacted in 1983) to the Equal Pay Act 1970. Directives create enforceable rights for employees against public sector employers, and individuals may be entitled to damages from the State if the government has not fully implemented a directive (Clarke 1994). The European Union has also issued resolutions, for instance on sexual harassment, and recommendations, for example on employment of and vocational training for disabled people. These are not binding on member states but may be used in tribunals and legal proceedings.

There is nothing comparable on race and disability. However, the European Convention on Human Rights and Fundamental Freedoms, which is enforced through the Court of Human Rights in Strasbourg, includes the right to enjoy its rights and freedoms without discrimination *on any grounds*. This includes race and disability, as well as sex, language and religion (Cooper and Vernon 1996). If the Court of Human Rights finds that United Kingdom law is failing to protect the Convention's rights, an Act of Parliament is necessary to change the law.

This European dimension is clearly illustrated in relation to sexuality. Reference is made throughout this book to the absence of UK legislation which expressly deals with discrimination on grounds of sexuality. However, the European Court of Justice has upheld a complaint of discrimination made by a transsexual who was dismissed when she underwent treatment for gender reassignment (P v. S *and Cornwall County Council* [1996]). The court found that the Equal Treatment Directive, which governs access to employment, promotion and working conditions, and vocational training, could not be confined simply to discrimination based on the fact that a person is one or other sex. The Directive is an expression of the principle of equality and applies therefore to discrimination based essentially if not exclusively on the sex of the individual concerned. Where discrimination arises from actual or potential gender reassignment of the individual concerned, he/she is treated unfairly by comparison with persons of the sex to which he/she was deemed to belong before undergoing gender reassignment. To tolerate such discrimination is a failure to respect the dignity and freedom to which the individual is entitled. Therefore, dismissal of a transsexual for reasons related to gender reassignment is contrary to the Equal Treatment Directive.

2:9	This ruling is immediately applicable to the public service sector where the Equal Treatment Directive is directly enforceable. Its application to private sector employers depends on whether the SDA 1975 may be construed to include discrimination for a reason related to gender reassignment. If not, that Act will have to be amended to comply with the ruling.
2:10	In another case currently before the European Court of Justice (*Lisa Grant v. South West Trains*), an employee complained of discrimination because her lesbian partner was refused the benefit of a travel pass. Had her partner been male, he would have been provided with a travel pass. In a preliminary opinion, the advocate general of the European Court of Justice has ruled that such discrimination cannot be justified. It breached European law guaranteeing equal pay, which includes benefits provided by an employer. As a matter of policy, therefore, discrimination on grounds of sexuality should be avoided.

Chapter 3
Signposts from administrative law

Three principles in particular may be discerned from administrative law, namely:
1 organisations must act legally and within their powers;
2 their procedures must be fair; and
3 the decisions reached must be reasonable.

The Ombudsman

Local authority policies, procedures and practice may be scrutinised by the Commissioner for Local Administration (Ombudsman). The Ombudsman may focus broadly on the administration of a case, investigating standards of decision-making and requiring a demonstration of fairness, an absence of bias, and due regard for procedures and legislative provisions. The investigative procedure can be lengthy and the Ombudsman has no power to enforce their suggested recommendations to rectify injustice arising from discrimination, incompetence, delay or other maladministration.

Quangos, other non-governmental organisations and government departments, including CCETSW, may find their administration subject to scrutiny by the Parliamentary Commissioner (Ombudsman). This Ombudsman is a possible source of redress for individuals.

Judicial review

Any public body can be subject to judicial review. In this procedure the court neither examines the merits or facts of a situation nor reappraises the case, but enquires into the decision-making process and its legality, procedural propriety and reasonableness. The focus is on whether an organisation has approached its decisions correctly. Have there been errors in law and/or procedures? Are the decisions (ir)rational given current law, procedures and considerations relevant to the case? Agencies must not act irrationally and must not manifestly fail to discharge their responsibilities. They have a duty to act fairly.

Judicial review can be a costly and lengthy procedure, for which legal advice is essential. Legal aid may be available. Leave (permission) to apply for judicial review must first be sought. This is normally an application by affidavit without an oral hearing. The criteria for granting leave are unclear, with wide variation in judicial practice, while individuals are less likely to reach or succeed at a final hearing than organisations (Dyer 1993).

Courts have criticised and discouraged the use of judicial review where there is an appropriate complaints or appeals procedure which could result in a speedier remedy, a mandate to consider the matter afresh, including the merits of the facts, and directions or recommendations to which the relevant authority must pay due regard. Any modifications to the recommendations coming out of a complaints procedure must not be unreasonable (R v North Yorkshire County Council, ex parte Hargreaves [1994]; R v Islington London Borough Council, ex parte Rixon [1996]). A failure to comply with the recommendations of a complaints procedure is not in itself a breach of the law, but the greater the departure the greater the need for cogent, articulated reasons if a court is subsequently not to infer that recommendations had been overlooked (R v Islington London Borough Council, ex parte Rixon [1996]).

Complaints procedures

People's reluctance to complain has been well documented (for example, Simons 1992; Buckley et al. 1995). It derives, at least in part, from the potential complainant's dependence on service provision and an associated fear of its loss; from their vulnerability, lack of confidence, and fear of damaging relationships; staff and organisational reluctance to endorse a person's right to complain; and scepticism about the outcome. Accordingly, the provision of a complaints procedure, of itself, is insufficient; people need to experience empowerment, and the organisation should actively promote accountability.

Studies of complaints procedures in welfare agencies (BASW 1989; SSI 1993; Dean and Hartley 1995; Simons 1995), and investigations by the Commissioner for Local Administration, have criticised arrangements for:
- inadequate publicity;
- time-scales incompatible with fairness and thoroughness;
- wording which discourages complainants;
- their concern with the performance of providers rather than the rights of the complainant;
- lack of access to an independent advocate for help in formulating

a complaint and/or resolving difficulties;
- failing to gather facts, record meetings, and give reasons for decisions;
- bias and an absence of fairness;
- failing to meet the needs of people from minority groups;
- not using outcomes to influence service development.

CCETSW's guidance (Skidmore 1995) on complaints procedures recommends that there should be an informal stage, reasonable time-scales, and clear terms of reference. Thus, where an independent person is involved in the hearing of a complaint, the meaning of the word "independent" should be clarified. The complainant should have the right to the support of a representative and the membership of the panel hearing a complaint should be balanced. The procedure should be accessible, with all students and applicants receiving copies of equal opportunity and anti-discriminatory policies, including action to be taken and procedures to be followed in the event of a complaint (Skidmore 1993). A named person, responsible for the procedure, should be clearly identified.

This advice parallels that given by the Department of Health (1990) to welfare agencies. Complaints should be resolved as quickly as possible, and as close to the service point as is acceptable. There should be an independent element. The procedure should be accessible, impartial and visible, and outcomes should inform service delivery. Complainants should have support. The operation of the procedure should be monitored.

The principle of the complainant having a representative, supporter and/or advocate has been endorsed by the courts (*McKenzie v McKenzie* [1970]). In civil and criminal proceedings anyone not legally represented may have assistance. This person may not address the court but may offer advice, take notes and sit beside the individual concerned.

Consultation with users

Administrative law has also set down principles for consultation with the users of a service when developments or changes are being proposed that would affect them. Organisations should consult before decisions have been made, that is when proposals are still at a formative stage. Reasons for the proposals should be given, and people should be given reasonable time to put their views. Individual needs and views should be taken into account in the decision-making process, and reasons should be given for the final decision (R v Devon County Council, ex parte Baker and Johns [1995]; R v Durham County Council, ex parte Curtis and Broxson [1995]).

Organisational competence

The implications of the foregoing paragraphs are that organisations must be administratively competent. This means, first, that they should consider what regulations and procedures might be required, perhaps by engaging in "what if ..." discussions. Secondly, the content and implementation of regulations and procedures should be discussed with all those to whom they might apply, in line with recommendations in the statutory codes of practice on employment (CRE 1984; EOC 1985). Such involvement helps to ensure that policies and procedures are known, understood and supported. This visible sharing of power and giving people a voice is a tangible expression of partnership and anti-discriminatory practice.

Thirdly, when writing policies and procedures, it is useful to distinguish (SSI, 1992; E. Davies, 1994) between:
- *philosophy* – the question why?, answered by reference to law and values, and demonstrating commitment, in this case to equal opportunities;
- *audit* – the assessment of the current position;
- *policy* – the question what?, generating aims and objectives;
- *strategy* – the question how?, generating action plans, and defining who is responsible;
- *tactics* – questions who?, what?, when? and how?, detailing implementation plans including training, recording, and publicity/dissemination to ensure that the policy is known;
- *procedures* – the question how?, giving guidance for day-to-day work; and
- *review* – auditing and monitoring implementation and effectiveness, as a prelude to resetting the policy and procedures.

Staff are more likely to understand, appreciate and absorb policy statements when they distinguish policy from operation. All the above elements must be present if organisations are to be able to say that their provision is accessible, appropriate, adequate and accountable (Butt *et al.* 1991).

However, adherence to good practice *diminishes* the closer one approaches operational reality (Booth *et al.* 1990): agreement on good practice is not necessarily implemented, particularly by those staff most affected. This highlights the importance of providing:
- accessible and visible procedures which set a clear and positive framework and which give guidelines and strength to those implementing and subject to them (E. Davies, 1994);
- adequate training for those involved in implementing the procedures;
- procedural clarity which addresses the complexities encountered by those operating the requirements; and
- texts which focus on anti-discriminatory practice, such as those produced by CCETSW as part of its Northern Curriculum Development Project (see Further Reading).

It should also be remembered that quality assurance returns to CCETSW are public records and, therefore, an encouragement to ensure that operational reality *is* good practice.

Chapter 4
The relationship between law and practice

The law is not unequivocal in its support for equal opportunities and anti-discriminatory practice. Some legislation is enabling, designed to challenge discrimination. The Sex Discrimination Act 1975, Race Relations Act 1976, and Welsh Language Act 1993 are examples, together with provisions in the Children Act 1989 (England and Wales), the Children (Scotland) Act 1995, and Children (NI) Order 1995 relating to race, culture, religion and language. The Criminal Justice Act 1991 (England and Wales only) also requires that those administering justice should be assisted through the publication of information to avoid discrimination. Other legislation, however, is overtly repressive: immigration controls and, in relation to homosexuality, provisions in the Local Government Act 1988 are examples. In other fields the law is silent, effectively conveying a message that "you do not exist". For instance, it is not unlawful to discriminate in employment on grounds of age. There is no legislation outlawing discrimination on grounds of HIV status although, once people with HIV develop symptoms indicative of a progressive condition, they will be covered by the provisions of the Disability Discrimination Act 1995 (Gooding 1996). The Race Relations Act 1976 does not cover religion. However, its indirect discrimination provisions may be helpful here (see paragraphs 5:2 and 5:4). Other than in Northern Ireland there is no legislation which outlaws discrimination on grounds of religion, yet sectarianism presents challenges for social workers in various parts of the UK, while holiday arrangements for students and employees usually reflect the Christian calendar (see paragraph 11:20).

Even where the law does provide a framework for combating discrimination in employment and service provision, and a means of redress, people's problems are individualised and the social attitudes and structural inequalities in which discrimination is rooted are not fundamentally challenged. The law in its present form does not effectively tackle the roots of discrimination. Rather, it focuses on the manifestations of discrimination, but this is not without its problems. Enforcement is difficult. Group actions are restricted, with each aggrieved individual having to press their own case rather than being joined to action already initiated by others in a similar position. Cost, the weakness of the available penalties and the track record of courts in understanding the needs and experiences of people from minority groups, together with the difficulty of proving discrimination, will deter some individuals from seeking redress. Industrial tribunals are able under section 56 of the RRA 1976; section 65 of the SDA 1975, and section 8 of the DDA 1995 to make practical recommendations to prevent further discrimination against an applicant, and to obviate or reduce the adverse effect on the complainant of the discriminatory act which is the subject of the complaint, but are often not asked to do so. Using the tribunal system, however, is not without its hazards for future employment prospects and, furthermore, compensates the victim without any guarantee of changing the workplace in which discrimination occurred. Again, difficulties of proof, together with the requirement to relive painful experiences when giving evidence, and the low success rate, act as deterrents. Finally, the powers of the Commission for Racial Equality and the Equal Opportunities Commission are limited, while the National Disability Council will not have any powers to investigate complaints or to enforce the provisions of the DDA 1995.

Moreover, reliance on the law alone is insufficient. The track record of welfare and justice agencies, for instance, in developing anti-discriminatory policies and services is unimpressive. Discrimination is still widespread in such areas as housing, education and health. Equal opportunities have not yet been realised (*The Guardian* 1992). Local authorities are more likely to have developed equal opportunity policies in relation to employment than initiatives to implement and monitor such policies. Most local authorities still need to develop equal opportunity service delivery policies, initiatives to implement them, and monitoring frameworks (Butt *et al.* 1991). Without effective sanctions the law is limited in its ability to change attitudes. Indeed, arguably, legislation has failed to secure a reduction in discrimination and has had little effect on inherited disadvantage (Banton 1994). However, improving the remedies available is only one part of the equation. Education, compulsory monitoring of employment and services, organisational commitment to address discrimination, and information provision are also necessary, in an effort to reduce the occasions when legal procedures may be required.

Not uncommonly the law provokes anxiety in those responsible for implementing its requirements, and is seen as a constraint or hindrance. Indeed, women, disabled people, and black people may point to its failure to support discrimination *for* them, as contrasted with outlawing discrimination *against* them (Cockburn 1991), and to tackle underlying structural inequalities. However, the law may also be seen as an opportunity for creating an expansive agenda for change. The task is to look for the room for manoeuvre.

The legislative framework upon which equal opportunity requirements are based is set out in Part 2. Its applicability is presented here in Table 1 for ease of reference.

Table 1: Legislative framework of equal opportunity requirements

	SDA 1975	RRA 1976	FE(NI) 1989	WLA 1993	DDA 1995
England	Yes	Yes	No	No	Yes
Northern Ireland	Yes*	No**	Yes	No	Yes
Scotland	Yes	Yes	No	No	Yes
Wales	Yes	Yes	No	Yes	Yes

* In separate Sex Discrimination (Northern Ireland) Order 1976.
** A separate Race Relations (Northern Ireland) Order 1997 has been issued.

Part 2

Equal opportunities and anti-discriminatory legislation

ACEGENDERLANGUAGE
ISABILITYEQUALOPPOR
UNITIESSEXUALITYLAW
UIDANCEPRACTICERACE
ENDERLANGUAGEDISA
ILITYEQUALOPPORTUN
IESSEXUALITYLAWGUID

Chapter 5
Race and gender
(1) Key provisions

The RRA 1976 applies to Great Britain but not to Northern Ireland while the SDA 1975 applies to both men and women. Both Acts, which mirror each other, are centrally concerned with employment and with service provision. Their key provisions are described here to set the scene and to define the boundaries of those provisions which apply directly to education and training.

Direct discrimination means treating a person less favourably than others are or would be treated in the same or similar circumstances. Less favourable treatment is prohibited on the grounds of sex and/or marital status (SDA 1975) or race, colour, nationality, including citizenship or ethnic or national origins (RRA 1976). Ethnic groups are defined by reference to two essential grounds, namely a long shared history and a cultural tradition of their own. They are further defined by a common language, literature, religion, and geographic origin, and by forming a minority or majority in a larger community (*Mandla v Dowell Lee* [1983]).

Under section 1(2) of the RRA 1976, segregation on racial grounds constitutes direct discrimination.

Indirect discrimination is often difficult to identify and goes undetected, hidden by long standing policy and practice. It consists of applying a requirement or condition which, although applied equally to all groups, has the effect of enabling a considerably smaller proportion of one particular racial group or people from one sex to comply with it, is detrimental to the individual concerned, and cannot be shown to be justifiable. Recruitment by word of mouth through the existing workforce is one example of indirect discrimination; another is setting an age or employment requirement for application to a post which has the effect of disadvantaging women who have taken career breaks in order to have children.

Whether a requirement or condition is justifiable is a question of fact which depends on the circumstances of each situation. An objective balance has to be struck between the discriminatory effect of the requirement and a reasonable need of the party applying the condition. The requirement must be justified objectively (*Hampson v. Department of Education and Science* [1989]). It is insufficient simply to assert a need for it.

GENDERLANGUA
ABILITYEQUALO
"UNITIESSEXUAL
VGUIDANCEPRA
RACEGENDERLA
GEDISABILITYEQ
PPORTUNITIESSE
ITYLAWGUIDAN
ACTICERACEGEN
ANGUAGEDISABI
QUALOPPORTUN

PART 2 : EQUAL OPPORTUNITIES AND ANTI-DISCRIMINATORY LEGISLATION

5:6	It is unlawful under section 39 of the SDA 1975 and sections 30 and 31 of the RRA 1976 for anyone to instruct or coerce other people to discriminate in ways prohibited by the RRA 1976 and SDA 1975. The giving of instructions or inducements to discriminate is unlawful.
5:7	It is unlawful under section 2 of the RRA 1976 and section 4 of the SDA 1975 to victimise by less favourable treatment people who bring proceedings, give evidence in proceedings, or allege discrimination under either act.
5:8	It is unlawful to discriminate in employment on grounds of sex and marital status, or race, colour, nationality, ethnic or national origins: ● in arrangements for recruitment and selection of candidates, including where adverts are placed; ● in terms on which employment is offered; ● by refusal or deliberate omission to offer employment; ● in opportunities for promotion, training, transfer or other benefits; ● by dismissal or other detriment.
5:9	Employers are liable for any discriminatory act performed by their employees, even if it is done without their knowledge and/or consent, unless they have taken all reasonably practicable steps to prevent such acts.
5:10	Where a positive action advertisement is used, it should not indicate or suggest an intention to discriminate. It should make clear that, while applications are particularly sought from one group, they are invited from all potential candidates. Positive action means encouraging one group but not discriminating against others. An advertisement may lawfully refer to a genuine occupational qualification, under sections 5 of the RRA 1976 and 7 of the SDA 1975 in particular circumstances. These sections allow someone from a particular racial group or sex to be appointed to provide personal services to promote the welfare of people from that same group or sex where these services can be provided most effectively by someone from that racial group or sex. Such action would not be lawful if the employer already had sufficient staff from that racial group or sex who can be employed on those duties. Employers would have to demonstrate that such an appointment represented more than just a preference, and that a personal service was being provided. Managerial or supervisory posts without such a personal

service element should not normally be advertised with a genuine occupational qualification (*Lambeth London Borough Council v* CRE [1990]). Both the RRA 1976 and the SDA 1975 permit a genuine occupational qualification where a job calls for authenticity (for example, acting or modelling). The SDA 1975 also permits such a qualification for jobs in single sex establishments.

| 5:11 | It could be lawful, therefore, for education and training providers to advertise for a black and/or woman consultant to provide counselling or support and advocacy to promote the welfare of black and/or women students, if these personal services could most effectively be provided by a black person or a woman. |

| 5:12 | Local authorities have a statutory duty (section 71 of the RRA 1976) to ensure that their functions are carried out with due regard to the need to eliminate unlawful racial discrimination and to promote equal opportunity and good relations between people of different racial groups. |

| 5:13 | It is unlawful under sections 20 of the RRA 1976 and 29 of the SDA 1975 for anyone who provides services, goods and facilities, including facilities for education and the services of a profession or any other public authority, to discriminate by refusing or omitting to provide them, or by the quality and manner in which they are provided. A failure to deal fairly and effectively with racial or sexual harassment may be a contravention of this requirement. However, section 35 of the SDA 1975 does allow services or facilities to be restricted to one sex where special care or attention is being provided, such as in hospital. |

Chapter 6
Race and gender
(2) Education and training provisions

Sections 17 of the RRA 1976 and 22 of the SDA 1975 make it unlawful to discriminate against a person, directly or indirectly, in the field of education. Sections 17 and 22 apply to admissions procedures, access to facilities and services, and treatment in such matters as exclusions and grant awards by local authorities. Similarly, sections 12 of the RRA 1976 and 13 of the SDA 1975 make it unlawful for an organisation which confers qualifications for professional practice to discriminate by refusing to provide a qualification or withdrawing it.

Both Acts apply to colleges in the further education sector through schedule 8 of the Further and Higher Education Act 1992 (paragraphs 75-88). They are required to promote good practice in education and employment, to monitor the effectiveness of their policies, and to take account of the needs of all groups who might experience discrimination.

Thus, one of the explicit criteria for approving S/NVQ assessment centres would be the ability to work within these legislative requirements, and to monitor access to training and awards to ensure they are free of barriers and discrimination. S/NVQs must be available to all who reach the required standard, must pay due regard to individuals' special needs, and must be assessed consistently.

Clearly, a prerequisite of these objectives is for inequality and discrimination to be identified in education and training, suggesting that providers should review all aspects of their provision. Phillipson (1992) refers to applying a gender lens to procedures and materials used. This may be extended to focusing on all possible forms of discrimination. For instance, to what extent do admissions procedures recognise the needs of black students? What positive statements are made in recruitment materials encouraging people from disadvantaged groups to apply? To what extent do curriculum materials convey only Eurocentric perspectives? Do they convey positive messages and images about, for example, disabled people? Are materials supplied in appropriate formats? To what extent are black students allocated to black tutors solely because of their race and ethnicity rather than particular defined and agreed needs?

Under section 35 of the RRA 1976, organisations may lawfully act to meet the special needs of persons of a racial group with regard to their education, training and welfare, by restricting access or allocating access first to members of a particular racial group. However, this group must have a special need which is attributable to and distinguished by a characteristic peculiar to that racial group, and which is met by such a restriction or special allocation (Home Office 1977; CRE 1985). Access courses may fall within section 35.

Where persons of a particular racial group or sex are under-represented in a particular work area in the workforce or in the population of the recruitment area, sections 37 and 38 of the RRA 1976 and 47 and 48 of the SDA 1975 permit training bodies and employers to encourage applications from persons of a particular racial group or sex, and to make training facilities available only to them, whether or not they are employees of the employer. There must, however, be a marked imbalance of people doing the type of work required. Training bodies and employers must be able to demonstrate under-representation, for example through research and community or workforce profiling. These sections also cover people who need training, having discharged domestic and family responsibilities to the exclusion of regular full-time paid employment. Selection decisions, however, must be made on merit.

Positive action may be taken by any education or training organisation, or employer, providing the criteria outlined above are met:
● to counter the persisting effects of discrimination and disadvantage, and
● to encourage applications from people under-represented in the workforce

The special training provisions are designed to enable them to qualify on merit for appointment and promotion.

According to the CRE (1985) positive action *is*:
● encouraging applications;
● offering training or retraining, to develop potential;
● offering mainstream career opportunities;
● setting targets for recruitment.

Positive action *is not*:
● lowering standards;
● applying quotas, or guaranteeing posts to those who have completed a positive action course, an example of unlawful

positive discrimination;
- selecting irrespective of merit, that is selecting on racial or gender grounds alone;
- applying genuine occupational qualifications, since jobs advertised using this provision (see paragraph 5:10) must meet certain specifications;
- separate funding for marginalised posts.

Positive action does not stop at the point of recruitment and selection. Successful applicants may experience isolation or be subjected to harassment or other forms of abuse and discrimination. Programme providers have a responsibility, therefore, to ensure that they provide effective support (see paragraph 15:5) to students throughout the programme. Failure to consider the implications for candidates of selection onto a programme, for instance in terms of assessment or group dynamics, constitutes discrimination by omission.

Chapter 7
Disability
(1) Key provisions

The Disability Discrimination Act 1995 differs in some fundamental respects from the legislation concerned with race and sex discrimination. There is no absolute prohibition of discrimination on grounds of disability, although the Act limits the circumstances where such discrimination is justifiable. The Act does not distinguish between direct and indirect discrimination, nor does it prohibit positive discrimination in favour of disabled people. This is because the Act does not apply to non-disabled people. It is lawful, therefore, for employers to advertise posts as only available to disabled people (Gooding 1996). However, local authorities are specifically prohibited from doing this.

Not all disabled people are covered, a point which organisations like RADAR have criticised. Disability is defined as 'a physical or mental impairment which has a substantial and long-term adverse effect on a person's ability to carry out normal day-to-day activities' (section 1). It must be long term (i.e. last at least 12 months) or be likely to recur (schedule 1). The Act defines normal activities in section 4 and mental impairment in schedule 1. The definition is further extended to cover people with fluctuating and/or progressive conditions and people whose disability is controlled by medication or involves severe disfigurement.

The definition of disability in the DDA 1995 is different from that which applies to assessment for and access to welfare services. That definition is to be found in the National Assistance Act 1948 (see paragraph 8:3).

The quota system for employment, created by the Disabled Persons (Employment) Act 1944, is abolished. The DDA 1995 prohibits less favourable treatment in employment of a person by reason of their disability if the employer cannot demonstrate that such treatment is justified (section 5). Such treatment is also prohibited if an employer fails to make a reasonable adjustment to the working environment and cannot justify that omission (section 6). Examples of what might constitute a reasonable adjustment are given in section 6. They include alteration to premises and working hours, assignment to different work, and the provision of assistance or training. The employment provisions (sections 5 and 6) only apply to organisations employing 20 people or more. The cost of the adjustments may be considered alongside the employer's resources when determining whether they are reasonable. Section 5 states that less favourable treatment will be justified only if it is material, that is relevant and significant to the circumstances of the case, and the reason is substantial. Clearly, then, a blanket policy, whether or not originating in stereotypes, would be unlawful.

The DDA 1995 (section 19) prohibits discrimination in access to and provision of goods and services (but not in transport or education). This means refusal of a service or less favourable treatment, which cannot be justified, for a reason relating to disability. Exceptions (section 20) include where:
- such access or provision would endanger the health and safety of a person;
- such access or provision would mean that other people could not have access or provision;
- less favourable treatment by reason of disability would allow a service to be provided to the disabled person or to others.

Section 18 requires providers to make reasonable adjustments, including the provision of aids and equipment. A code of practice is now available (NDC 1996a) (see paragraph 2:3).

Section 55 prohibits victimisation of a person who initiates proceedings, or gives evidence in proceedings, or makes an allegation within the terms of the Act.

Advertisements for jobs which indicate an intent to discriminate against disabled people are not prohibited. However, under section 11, advertisements indicating that a disabled person might be at a disadvantage or that an employer would not willingly make reasonable adjustments may result in a tribunal which could conclude that the non-appointment of a disabled person was a result of their disability. This has been criticised (Gooding 1996) as insufficient protection for a disabled person, because an employer could still argue that the employment decision was justified within the terms of the Act.

The DDA 1995 has drawn substantial criticisms from organisations of disabled people, and others. It fails, they argue, to address social attitudes and structural relationships which disable people. Indeed, it compounds disadvantage by vagueness in drafting, weakness in some of its employment and services provisions, and by emphasising, as with welfare legislation for disabled people, needs and resources rather than rights.

The DDA 1995 is being introduced in stages, accompanied by regulations and guidance. A code of good practice on the employment of disabled people (Department of Employment Group 1984) provides guidance about recruitment of disabled people and assisting disabled people at work. This code needs to be read alongside the regulations and guidance designed to implement the DDA 1995 (NDC 1996b). Both documents encourage employers to avoid making assumptions, to consider the need for specialist advice, and to plan ahead. They outline the extent to which employers must consider making alterations to premises and employment practices to assist in the recruitment and retention of disabled employees, and detail an equal opportunity approach to recruitment.

A guide for disabled people on employment rights has been issued by RADAR (1992). Again, this pre-dates the DDA 1995. However, it refers to industrial tribunal cases which have helped to define the responsibilities of employers when recruiting disabled people or when making decisions about their future employment. It also identifies cases which cast light on how employers will be expected to implement the requirements of the new legislation.

The Health and Safety at Work Act 1974 imposes a duty on employers to provide a safe work place, including means of access and exit, for *all* employees.

Chapter 8
Disability
(2) Education and training provisions

Education is specifically excluded from the DDA 1995 requirement (section 19) on providers not to discriminate by reason of disability in the provision of goods and services. Nor does the Act require educational institutions to become accessible (Gooding 1996). It is left to further and higher education funding councils to determine the degree to which institutions will promote access by disabled students to their training programmes.

Section 30 requires further education institutions to provide information about the accessibility of their facilities. They will be required to furnish an annual statement giving details of their progress in providing facilities and their future plans. Colleges in Scotland already have to provide such information. Higher education institutions will be required to provide statements on how they are meeting and intend to meet the needs of disabled students. Similar requirements will be enacted in Northern Ireland, consequent upon changes in its further and higher educational structure. Depending on the exact content of forthcoming regulations, these statements are likely to include information on access, equipment, admission policies and procedures, and student welfare services.

If a student is disabled within the meaning of disability given in section 29 of the National Assistance Act 1948 (in Northern Ireland, section 1 of the Chronically Sick and Disabled Persons (NI) Act 1978), they may request an assessment under the Disabled Persons Act 1986 (in Northern Ireland, Disabled Persons (NI) Act 1989). The assessment is designed to establish the need for services under section 2 of the Chronically Sick and Disabled Persons Act 1970 (in Northern Ireland, Chronically Sick and Disabled Persons (NI) Act 1978). The definition of disability in the National Assistance Act 1948 covers blind and partially sighted people, deaf people, people with speech impairments, people with a mental disorder, and disabled people. The definition applies to children and young people as well as adults needing care or services. The services listed include the provision of assistance in taking advantage of educational facilities, including those outside the local authority's area (LAC(93)12). Such assistance could include funding by the local authority of personal care required to enable a student to pursue their studies. The link between needs and resources in relation to this legislation is complicated (see Preston-Shoot 1996) but in essence, once a local authority has accepted that a need exists for which it must provide services, then resources cannot be used as a reason for avoiding that obligation. However, resources may be relevant to a judgement about need, which is a relative term, expressed usually through eligibility criteria. The exercise of discretion, and the weight given to resources, in determining such criteria, must be reasonable (R v *Gloucestershire County Council and Another, ex parte Barry* [1997]).

Section 8 of the Chronically Sick and Disabled Persons Act 1970 and Chronically Sick and Disabled Persons (NI) Act 1978 require all new educational buildings to make provision, in so far as practicable and reasonable in the circumstances, for access to and within the building, including parking facilities and toilets. Part M of building regulations requires access for disabled people in new buildings, including offices and public buildings, and reasonable toilet provision. Student accommodation is exempt as it is classed as residential accommodation.

Disabled students on full time courses in higher education such as the DipSW, including students with learning disabilities and dyslexia, may be eligible for up to three disabled student allowances as part of their mandatory award. These allowances, to assist students to meet essential costs related to their course, are for:
- a non-medical helper (a signer or proof reader, for example, available annually);
- major items of equipment (available once only);
- a general allowance to cover minor items of equipment such as tapes and Braille paper; and
- other costs incurred as a result of the disability (available annually).

For those on further education courses, including programmes which prepare students for vocational qualifications and access to higher education courses, such support is at the discretion of the grant awarding body. Medical or other evidence, for instance from an educational psychologist, may be required.

The grants are unlikely to be adequate. Students cannot assume that all their needs will be met through these allowances or that they will cover the full cost of necessary support. The rates of the allowances, and the rules governing their operation, are liable to annual variation. The allowances are subject to a means test, representing a tax on disability. Concern has also been expressed that authorities

make subjective decisions about the allowances, and that the process of application is demeaning, stressful and time consuming (James and Thomas 1996). For non-graduates, these are available from:
● local education authorities in England and Wales;
● education and library boards in Northern Ireland;
● Scottish Office education department, student awards agency.

For graduates, the grants are available from:
● CCETSW, through its bursary scheme, in England, Wales and Scotland;
● DHSS in Northern Ireland.

Sections 5 and 6 of the Disabled Persons Act 1986 require local education authorities in England and Wales to notify social services departments of the future plans of disabled young people, when they are approaching the end of their compulsory education. This is to assist social services departments in their assessment of a person's potential need for welfare services. Similar provisions apply in Scotland and Northern Ireland. When a young person moves into further education, the relevant educational institution has a duty to notify the social services department of the date that person is expected to leave full-time education.

Guidance issued by the National Council for Vocational Qualifications advises that NVQ awarding bodies and assessment centres must pay due regard to the special needs of individuals, including those with physical or sensory disabilities, or learning difficulties. In particular, disabled students may require assistance and support to undertake assessment.

The implications of this chapter are that programme providers should monitor their procedures and consult with disabled people on their effectiveness. Thus, to what extent are disabled people clearly informed of the people to approach for advice and support? What guidance and training is given to staff involved in recruitment and selection decisions? How does this guidance and training address the assumptions and stereotypes which may be held about disabled people entering social work and social care courses and employment, and which may prejudice decisions about the recruitment and progression of disabled people? How adequate are the arrangements made to enable disabled students to complete the curriculum and the assessments?

Chapter 9
Fair employment and race relations legislation in Northern Ireland

Northern Ireland has its own fair employment legislation. Section 16 of the Fair Employment (NI) Act 1976, as amended by section 49 of the Fair Employment (NI) Act 1989, prohibits both direct and indirect discrimination. Section 20 of the Fair Employment (NI) Act 1989 seeks to secure equal opportunities between people of different religious (and no religious) and political beliefs when seeking or in employment and when seeking or being engaged in an occupation. Section 20 also includes training for an occupation provided by any person.

Both Acts prohibit less favourable treatment. For instance, when providing services in connection with training for employment or an occupation, it is unlawful under section 22 of the 1976 Act to discriminate by refusing services, or by the way services are offered, or in the terms offered. It is unlawful under section 23 of the 1976 Act for people with the power to confer qualifications to discriminate. Section 58 of the 1989 Act permits employers to implement affirmative action policies. Section 37 of the 1976 Act prohibits discrimination by training programmes, but under section 53 of the 1989 Act affirmative action is lawful.

The 1989 Act, which created a Fair Employment Commission, is the most radical equal opportunity statute in the UK (Taylor, 1992). This is because it makes monitoring a statutory requirement, and requires rather than simply permits affirmative action. Specifically, it imposes duties on employers to:
- review their workforce composition and applications on grounds of gender and religion;
- review composition and recruitment, training and promotion practices at least every three years;
- take affirmative action if fair participation is not being secured by members of the different communities;
- set goals and timetables as part of affirmative action.

The 1989 Act is also radical in the area of contract compliance. Public authorities are obliged to require firms with whom they contract for goods and services to comply with this legislation.

The Fair Employment Commission has the power to investigate complaints of discrimination against employers, organisations conferring qualifications for employment, and organisations providing services for training for employment or an occupation. It may seek a resolution of such complaints, and make recommendations where necessary. It may examine work practices, implement monitoring procedures and set goals and timetables in relation to employers (with more than 10 employees) who must register with the Commission (Gibson *et al.* 1994). The Commission may publish a code of practice on the promotion of equal opportunities. Sections 16 of the 1976 Act and 46 of the 1989 Act make the principles of the code mandatory, but failure to observe it is not an offence.

Individuals may take complaints of discrimination in employment to a Fair Employment Tribunal which has the power to specify remedial action and to compensate victims. For other complaints, access to redress is through the civil courts.

The Race Relations (Northern Ireland) Order 1997 parallels the Race Relations Act 1976 with which, therefore, it shares the same strengths and weaknesses. It prohibits direct and indirect discrimination, and victimisation against people who initiate proceedings under its provisions. The Order prohibits discrimination by employers in selection arrangements, in the terms of employment offered, and with respect to access to promotion, training, facilities and services. It prohibits discrimination by authorities and bodies which confer authorisation or provide qualifications to practise, and those people or bodies who provide or make arrangements for the provision of vocational training. They must not discriminate in access to or withdrawal from training, and in the way training is delivered. Additionally, the Order makes it unlawful for educational establishments to discriminate in access to facilities and services or in the way that they are provided. People providing goods, facilities and services to the public must not discriminate in the manner of provision or by refusing to supply. The Order outlaws discriminatory advertisements and pressure to discriminate.

As in the Race Relations Act 1976, the Order allows for "Genuine Occupational Qualifications" (see paragraph 5:10). Similarly, it also establishes that employers are liable for the actions of their employees unless they can demonstrate that they have taken all reasonably practicable steps to prevent discrimination. There are parallel provisions for positive action in respect of access to facilities and services, and to education and training, to meet the specific education, training and welfare needs of racial groups.

The Order creates a Commission for Racial Equality (Northern Ireland) with powers to issue a code of practice, to conduct investigations, to make recommendations, and to issue non-discrimination notices. Individuals with complaints may seek redress through industrial tribunals for employment matters, and through the civil courts for other concerns.

Chapter 10
The Welsh Language Act 1993

The Welsh Language Act (WLA) 1993 requires all public bodies in Wales to have a Welsh Language Policy and their language schemes must be approved by the Welsh Language Board (WLB). The WLB is responsible for promoting and facilitating the use of the Welsh language, in line with the Act's requirement that the Welsh language is to be treated equally, where appropriate and practicable, with the English language. It is responsible for ensuring that public bodies, as defined in section 6, prepare a language scheme. Public bodies include CCETSW, local authorities in Wales, and institutions of further and higher education.

When preparing a language scheme, public bodies should consult with Welsh speakers and indicate how they intend to implement the scheme within the provision of their services. They should indicate how they intend to ensure the equal status of Welsh with English, and their timetable for action. Organisations in other sectors are encouraged to develop policies.

The WLB may investigate non-compliance on its own initiative, and, on receipt of a complaint, may enquire into a public body's failure to implement their scheme. Such a complaint is the only formal mechanism open to would-be complainants. If a public body refuses to implement its recommendations, the WLB may refer the matter to the Secretary of State for Wales who may seek a court injunction (E. Davies, 1994).

The WLA 1993 has been criticised for not covering the entire public sector, such as government departments, and for omitting the private and voluntary sectors (G.P. Davies, 1994). Furthermore, it does not extend to individuals the right to speak Welsh when dealing with public bodies such as social services departments. It does, however, endorse the principle that Welsh is the only medium for providing a linguistically appropriate service to all users. It may, therefore, be seen as an appropriate extension of commitments in social welfare and justice legislation to young people, adults needing care or services, and offenders.

The relationship between the WLA 1993 and the RRA 1976 has been confused. This is because the Government rejected a clause which would have clarified that a Welsh language requirement for employment was permissible if the post holder regularly interacted with Welsh speakers, if proficiency in the Welsh language was only at a level required to perform the work, and if a facility was offered to learn Welsh (G.P. Davies, 1994). Without this clarification, and since individuals do not have the right to speak Welsh when dealing with public bodies (see paragraph 10:4), organisations have had to include within their schemes details of how the requirements of the WLA 1993 (see paragraph 10:4) will be met. They also have to state how services will be delivered that support the equal treatment of Welsh and English.

However, the WLB in consultation with the CRE (1996) has issued advice that:
● where linguistic ability is considered essential or desirable for any post, this should be specified in recruitment;
● a linguistic condition or requirement is justifiable where research and a Welsh language scheme conclude that Welsh speakers are needed for an organisation to meet its obligations under the Welsh Language Act 1993; and
● where a non-Welsh speaker is appointed to a post for which ability to speak Welsh is considered essential, a condition of employment should be to learn the language to the required level of proficiency within a reasonable, agreed period, with agency support.

Thus, organisations must consider the relevance of linguistic ability to a post, and base such judgements on objective criteria and the skills necessary. The provision of Welsh language training should, therefore, form part of any scheme. This guidance is designed to ensure that the public have access to sufficient and appropriately skilled Welsh speakers, to enable workplaces to deliver a full service through the medium of Welsh. Thus, Welsh language schemes should identify posts where the ability to speak Welsh is considered essential or desirable in order to deliver a full service, and to what level of proficiency, and for what reasons. The scheme, and the available numbers of Welsh speakers, should be monitored in order to determine if advertised posts should include the ability to speak Welsh as either essential or desirable.

CCETSW has a Welsh language policy based on equal status for Welsh and English, and the right to choose language as central to good practice. All programmes, and the institutions in which they are based, must have a policy and strategy for the implementation of Welsh medium training and learning opportunities.

The implications for CCETSW and for programmes of education and training of the WLA 1993, and other legislation referred to previously, will be discussed in Part 3. Stewart Collins *et al.* (1997) have provided details of how one DipSW programme has responded to the requirements of the WLA 1993 with respect to rights for students, the status of the Welsh language, and choice for Welsh language students. They note the slow progress in guaranteeing Welsh speakers a service in the language of their choice, and the importance of not placing responsibility on the student/service user for access to appropriate provision.

Part 3

Application of the legislation in specific areas

Chapter 11
Entry into education and training programmes

Direct discrimination

Discrimination by any training body on grounds of religion (in Northern Ireland), race, or sex and marital status is unlawful under sections 13 of the RRA 1976, 14 of the SDA 1975, 21-23 of the Fair Employment (NI) Act 1976, 20 of the Fair Employment Act (NI) 1989 and 14 of the Race Relations (NI) Order 1997. They cannot discriminate in the terms on which they admit people onto a training course, or by refusing to admit a person or terminating a place on these grounds. Discrimination by an educational establishment on grounds of race, sex or religion is similarly unlawful under sections 17 of the RRA 1976, 22 of the SDA 1975, 22-23 of the Fair Employment (NI) Act 1976, 20 of the Fair Employment Act (NI) 1989, and section 18 of the Race Relations (NI) Order 1997. They cannot discriminate in the terms set for entry and admission, in the way access to services and facilities is offered, and by refusing to accept applications.

It follows that the imposition of quotas is unlawful. It would also be unlawful for requirements not applied to other candidates to be imposed on candidates from a particular group. These might include additional qualification requirements, writing or articulation skills, or experience. This guidance is also applicable to the allocation of bursaries to candidates registering with post qualifying consortia.

Indirect discrimination

Indirect discrimination would arise, however, if academic criteria (such as writing skills) were set as conditions, if they exceeded the knowledge and skills required to demonstrate an ability to complete the programme of study, and this would effectively exclude a higher number of students from one group, and if the criteria could not be justified on educational grounds.

Indirect discrimination would arise if non-academic criteria were set as conditions and could not be justified on educational grounds and would exclude a higher proportion of students from one group who might, otherwise, be suitable. Length of experience in paid or voluntary work would come into this category since, for example, it might exclude women who have previously been full-time family carers.

To avoid allegations of indirect discrimination, any requirement set as an entry condition for a programme or as a criterion for allocation of a bursary (see paragraph 11:2) must be *objectively justifiable on educational grounds* (see paragraph 5:5). For instance, a requirement for particular levels or types of experience must be justifiable in the context of the programme of study in all the circumstances of the case, balancing its discriminatory effects against the discriminator's "need" for it (*Ojutiku and Oburoni v Manpower Services Commission* [1982]; *Hampson v. Department of Education and Science* [1989]). Where programmes wish to specify that candidates should have some paid or unpaid experience in a social work or social care setting, this must be justifiable in terms of the length of the course, the number and type of placements provided, and understanding of the nature of social work. The requirement should not be expressed as a blanket policy in order to allow for appropriate exceptions.

Similarly, procedures used to determine a candidate's suitability must be fair, to avoid discrimination in the way access to facilities is offered. Thus, interview questions and written tests must avoid cultural bias and must be capable of justification on educational grounds. For example, where a written test is used to determine understanding of social work or levels of language, communication and comprehension skills, the standard required for safe and effective performance as a (student) social worker should be made clear. Put another way, the elements of any selection procedure should be relevant to the training offered and should be capable of assessing objectively a person's ability to undertake the training and, if successful, to gain and perform satisfactorily in appropriate employment.

Evidence exists (see for instance, Mallinson and Best 1990; Burgess *et al.* 1992) that black applicants have to prove competence while white candidates' competence is accepted unquestioningly, and that black applicants are more likely to be questioned critically. Questions asked should relate to, and only test, genuine requirements for training. The scoring and decision-making mechanisms used should be free from unjustifiable bias, based on clear criteria relating to a person specification and job description, relate to a candidate's actual performance, and contain reasons for the decisions made.

Age discrimination

It is not unlawful to discriminate on grounds of age. However, it is possible that age discrimination could be an indirect form of discrimination on grounds of race or sex. This might arise where age was used as an absolute disqualification and if the proportion of people from one group who could apply was considerably smaller than other groups similarly qualified (Jones v University of Manchester [1993]). Thus, age limits should only be employed where they are necessary and can be justified educationally in the context of the training provided. They should be questioned when applied to access to training and promotion (Malone 1993). There is no minimum entry age for the DipSW so students can start at any age provided they are successful in gaining a place. However, the social work training rules (CCETSW 1996) state that students must have reached their twenty-second birthday in order to receive their certificate. Students completing programmes who are under this age will not receive their DipSW certificates until they turn 22 and their qualification will be marked with this date.

Sexuality and discrimination

There is no UK legislation prohibiting discrimination on grounds of sexuality (but refer to paragraphs 2:8-2:10). However, there would be direct sex discrimination if a person enquired about sexual orientation of male applicants and rejected applications from gay men, but failed to make similar enquiries of female applicants (Malone 1993). Sex discrimination might also arise if, for reasons which could not be justified educationally in relation to the programme of study, different criteria were applied between homosexual men and women because of stereotypical assumptions about the suitability of some people for work in the caring professions. There should be no pressure on students to disclose their sexuality.

Person specification and job description

One key to ensuring openness and fairness, and to promoting an equal opportunity approach to entry, is a person specification which identifies the necessary skills, knowledge and experience, and a job description which clarifies duties, responsibilities and roles. These must be clear on the qualities and requirements sought in applicants. Once listed, essential attributes can be assessed in observable and measurable ways through set questions and tasks related to suitability for the programme of study. They will then provide information on the extent to which applicants meet the specified qualities and requirements. An applicant's performance can then be scored against these attributes, with clearly defined criteria to guide the allocation of a score. Full details can be sent to prospective applicants, in appropriate formats (such as language or tape).

Discriminatory questions must be avoided. Equally, the questions asked and the interpretation by interviewers of the answers should be monitored for bias and assumptions, for example about ambition, careers and gender roles. As a guideline, questions and any selection procedures should be specifically related to the requirements of training and should assess an applicant's ability to train for social work (EOC 1988). Where it is necessary to assess whether personal circumstances will affect performance in training (for example, where placements might involve extensive travel or working unsocial hours), this should be discussed with all candidates and without questions which make assumptions about marital status, children and domestic obligations. Clearly, any paper and interview selection should be monitored to ensure that candidates are encouraged to identify the relevance of the situations and experiences they have encountered, and to show their reflection on and learning from them. In particular, assessment of prior experience, including the accreditation of prior learning and experience, must not be so tightly drawn that it excludes or is to the detriment of either men or women or any racial group (CRE/EOC 1995). The monitoring will seek to ensure that programmes do not limit their intake to candidates with 'usual' experience or career profiles.

The job (training) description will:
- concentrate on job (training) demands;
- provide a factual list of responsibilities, duties or tasks, and level and location of accountability;
- be written in clear and gender-neutral language;
- refer to additional information – the person specification, description of the agency where the programme of study is located, procedures which govern the programme of study, rights of students;
- omit any reference to personal characteristics.

The person specification will:
- be based on the job (training) description;
- focus on attributes and actual requirements needed by the person

as student, namely essential minimum standards without which an applicant will be rejected, and desirable additional elements which would improve a person's effectiveness and performance as a student;
- avoid making assumptions about "the right person to be a student";
- avoid attributes which are not justifiable by reference to the job description, or which cannot be tested;
- avoid unnecessary inflation of particular attributes which are included, that is avoid prioritising any one attribute.

Each criterion in the person specification should be capable of objective justification against the requirements of the post, thus ensuring non-discriminatory treatment of candidates.

The person specification will concentrate on four areas:
1 experience, specifying the amount, nature, and level but allowing for transferable skills (for example, unpaid caring responsibilities as opposed to voluntary work or paid employment);
2 education qualifications which can be justified;
3 knowledge and skills, distinguishing between what is required now and what can be learned;
4 other factors which are a regular feature of training and closely related to study for a qualification.

Positive action on race and gender

What positive action, then, is allowable on race and gender? In addition to earlier comments in paragraphs 6:7 and 6:8, positive action is:
- providing training and encouragement to under-represented groups to equip them with the skills and experience necessary for a successful application and subsequent performance – for example, training to equip workers with the necessary skills and experience for a DipSW application;
- providing at least one interviewer drawn from the racial group of the interviewee, and ensuring that women are not interviewed just by men, but equally ensuring that black interviewers also interview white applicants, and women interview men;
- employing a consultant to establish training for people in interviewing skills for potential DipSW applicants;
- monitoring applications to identify areas of under-representation,

to consider whether this reflects direct or indirect discrimination, and to take appropriate positive action in response (CRE 1985);

● advertising widely to reach under-represented groups, while demonstrating care in the placement of advertisements to ensure that all communities are reached;

● recruitment materials translated into other languages;

● creating links with community groups and voluntary agencies in order to encourage applications (CRE/EOC 1995);

● selection by employers for training of people from groups under-represented in their workforce or in comparison with the area population;

● setting targets which could reasonably be expected in an equal opportunity process (CRE 1992).

These last two elements require community mapping and an adequate knowledge of the workforce, primarily for two reasons. First, to ensure that the training, facilities and services available are appropriate. Secondly, to ensure that targets set for recruitment are not based on 'thin air' or 'think of a number and double it', but are rooted in knowledge of the local communities (size, age, needs, structure), national workforce and population statistics, and indicators of need for services. It is, therefore, good practice to consult relevant local service and community organisations and groups, and to evaluate the responses of recruited students to policies and practice.

Positive action does not include making discriminatory selection decisions on grounds of race or sex in order to reach targets. Nor is it about discriminating at the point of recruitment. But it does raise questions about how to make fair selection decisions. Where students have been scored against clear selection criteria, places should be allocated according to score. Where students have achieved identical scores and where there are fewer places available than students with this identical score, it is unlawful to prioritise women over men, or black students over white students. Selection in this situation should be on the basis of 'names out of a hat'.

Underpinning good practice

Interviewers should point out to *all* applicants that CCETSW has an Equal Opportunities Policy which demands commitments from training providers and students and that the training agency has policies on equal opportunities and harassment. They also have a responsibility to explore all applicants' commitment and ability to implement that policy and underpinning value base.

Good practice in recruitment and selection should be underpinned by:
- a published code of practice;
- training on legislative provisions and the development of an equal opportunity approach to interviewing for all those involved;
- records of the reasons for decisions taken which allow candidates to receive feedback; and
- monitoring, including questionnaires to successful and unsuccessful candidates, summaries of complaints, and reports on how the findings have been used to revise procedures and inform targets. Monitoring may also include scrutiny, for example by S/NVQ training and assessment centres, of the number of individuals from minority groups employed by particular local authorities in comparison with local and national profiles, contrasting this with the registration and completion rates of S/NVQ candidates.

Helpful recruitment strategies include:
- information days held on site and in local communities;
- use of video material which includes participation by black and disabled students; and
- workshops for potential candidates which provide information about the course, the support it provides, the area in which it is located, and the agencies with which it collaborates.

Once candidates have been selected, training providers should then consider the composition of the group and identify what supports people from minority groups might need. Ideally, these matters should be discussed with participants before or at the outset of the programme, rather than left until problems arise. For example, employers and employees may agree time off for religious festivals, and arrangements for religious practice at work. Training programmes should also consider such arrangements.

Chapter 12
Criminal convictions and suitability for professional social work

There is evidence of considerable discrimination against offenders (Clarke 1994), with blanket prejudice replacing selection on merit. Therefore, in devising an equal opportunity policy, consideration must be given to including ex-offenders in equal opportunity statements and recruitment guidelines.

The decision about whether or not to admit an ex-offender onto a training programme can create difficulties. First, if a DipSW programme accepts a student, it is responsible for delivering the education and training required. If the programme is subsequently unable to deliver any part of a programme, say because the student has a conviction and cannot be placed, the student may have a remedy through the courts for breach of contract (Skidmore 1993). Secondly, views differ widely about what offences might constitute an absolute disqualification. Some offences, particularly those involving violence and abuse, including financial abuse, might be taken to indicate doubts about the trustworthiness fundamental to a practitioner-client relationship. However, blanket policies risk overlooking the individual circumstances of particular cases.

Applicants with criminal convictions underline the need for competent administration (see paragraph 3:13). Criminal convictions may be disclosed at interview or come to light subsequently. A training programme therefore requires a procedure consistent with the policies of, and agreed with the partner agencies, which addresses both the actual offence and instances of any failure to disclose, either at all or in full.

Section 1 of the Rehabilitation of Offenders Act 1974 establishes that a criminal record may become "spent" and, thereafter, treated as if it had not happened. The length of time varies according to the sentence (section 5). Once "spent", a candidate for employment does not have to reveal the offence and it cannot be used as a ground for dismissal or refusal to appoint (section 4). A person with "spent" convictions has a right under section 3 not to be discriminated against in employment – in promotion, and the provision of training, benefits, services and facilities. There is no general duty to disclose "unspent" convictions (section 4) but they should be declared to an employer on request. Dishonesty at that point could be grounds for dismissal (subject to the restrictions relating to "spent" convictions) depending on the circumstances, the person's employment record, the nature of the offence, and its relationship to the post. The procedure to be followed in such instances must be shown to be fair.

Under section 4(4) and LAC(93)17 there are exceptions to the procedure whereby spent convictions do not have to be disclosed. These include social services department employees, health care workers and youth workers. They can be asked to reveal 'spent' convictions and may be refused employment or be dismissed because of a conviction or a failure to disclose it.

The relevant circular (LAC(93)17), issued under section 7 of the Local Authority Social Services Act 1970 (see paragraph 2:2), requires a senior nominated officer in a local authority to request a police check on people employed or otherwise directly engaged by them (such as foster parents). The circular, which also applies to social work students, covers work which will give people substantial unsupervised access on a sustained and regular basis to children under the age of 16 (18 if they have special needs). It provides guidelines on 'substantial unsupervised access' which means appreciable time without another responsible adult present; greater vulnerability when a child is away from home and regular contact. The circular recommends that police forces should aim to reply within 10 days unless enquiries have to be made of other forces, when the target set is three weeks.

A person with a criminal conviction, the circular acknowledges, is not automatically rendered unsuitable for work with children. The circular, therefore, recommends that a judgement is made as to suitability which takes into account those offences which may be relevant to the situation in question. In each case, the nature of the offences, the nature of the appointment, the date of the offences and frequency of offending should be considered. Thus, while a programme may agree with its partners the nature and type of offences which might render a person unsuitable for (or to continue with) training, each individual situation should be fully considered and the reasons recorded for decisions reached.

The scope of protection for vulnerable people is more extensive in Northern Ireland where people with learning disabilities are covered (DHSS (NI) 1989).

Since social work students must undertake two placements in appropriate agencies, training programmes must agree procedures with placement providers in order to ensure that students with criminal convictions who are allowed onto the programme can complete the requirements. To avoid potential liability, programmes should ask students, having fully appraised them of the Rehabilitation of Offenders Act 1974, to sign a declaration disclosing any convictions before they are offered a place. They should explain the significance of non disclosure and of any offences which emerge after selection, and should clarify that the offer of a place is subject to any discussions which are necessary in the light of disclosure or non disclosure. Students should provide proof of identity in order to ensure that the name given when requesting a police check is accurate.

Whatever procedure is established for deciding whether a student can be admitted onto, or continue with a programme, there must be due process which means a right:
● to be heard;
● to have the individual circumstances of the case considered in spite of the presence of outline categories of offences which would normally disqualify;
● to challenge evidence;
● to be accompanied by a McKenzie friend (see paragraph 3:11); and
● to be given reasons for decisions.

Where a student is being prosecuted but has not yet been convicted, depending on the nature of the alleged offence and charge, it may be necessary to advise them to withdraw temporarily from the programme unless arrangements can be made to protect colleagues and clients (CCETSW 1993). The question should be considered using procedures similar to those for investigating disclosure or non-disclosure of a conviction.

The training rules (CCETSW 1996) place a requirement on DipSW programme partnerships to ensure that all students admitted or recommended for award of the qualification are suitable to become social workers. Procedures should contain a clause which recognises that there may be circumstances (such as professional misconduct) in which information comes to light which appears to question a person's suitability to hold a professional qualification. A panel, appropriately constituted in terms of race and gender, should be established to investigate the information. This will involve receiving information, questioning those involved, and making recommendations to the programme. The clause and procedure should be published and should contain a right of appeal on the usual grounds, namely that regulations have not been followed and/or that information, which might have led to a different decision, was not available at the time the decision was reached.

Chapter 13
Disabled students and entry into training

As identified in chapters 5 and 6, the Disability Discrimination Act 1995 differs from other anti-discriminatory legislation by not prohibiting positive discrimination in favour of disabled people in certain circumstances, or discrimination by employers on the basis of disability, again in certain circumstances. As also identified, education and training is excluded from the actual provisions concerning anti-discrimination in relation to the provision of goods and services. The net result is that the scope for positive action may be greater, providing that whatever action is taken does not conflict with the provisions of other anti-discriminatory legislation. However, disabled applicants have fewer safeguards built into the legislation against the terms of entry set by training bodies and educational institutions.

More positively, the DDA 1995 does contain provisions which offer useful guidelines for training programmes as to the obligations on potential and actual employers in respect of disabled people (see paragraph 7:4) and on providers of services (see paragraph 7:5). Thus, the focus should be on what applicants can do, on their abilities rather than disability, and on how their potential can be maximised. Selection criteria should be justifiable on educational grounds and relate to the programme of study and the occupation for which a qualification is being sought. Blanket exclusions should be avoided (as in applications for employment), with exclusion having to be justified in each individual case based on an assessment of abilities (Gooding 1996). Where job descriptions are used, they should be compiled as unrestrictively as possible. Job and career prospects should be assessed flexibly and the different ways to do the same job effectively should be recognised. Where necessary, aids for daily living should be considered and job tasks restructured (DEG 1984).

Programme providers should establish links with careers advisers, local groups of disabled people, access courses, and job centres, both to advertise their provision and to dispel myths about the suitability of disabled people for work in health care, social care, and social work. This active encouragement of applications should form part of a statement of intent to encourage disabled students into training. The outcome, in terms of applications, selection, and progress through training programmes, can then be monitored. Recent research suggests that these links are rarely established and that information provided by programmes does not encourage disabled people to apply (Walker 1995) since it tends to highlight problems rather then how potential can be maximised.

Disabled applicants should be given copies of the reports compiled by academic institutions concerning access and the facilities they provide (see paragraph 8:2) so that they may assess how far their needs might be met. Institutions should openly acknowledge any barriers. These reports, and any other information provided, should be in appropriate formats (Braille, tape, video with sign language), similar to the requirements in section 9 of the Disabled Persons Act 1986 concerning the provision of information by social services departments.

Criteria for shortlisting should not introduce unnecessary requirements that may exclude disabled people, and should cover transferable skills and experiences which may have developed in alternative situations and may compensate for any fragmented work profile (EL(95)143). Interview procedures should incorporate arrangements required to assist disabled applicants, namely appropriate venue, facilities to meet the requirements of any written test, and facilitators at interviews (interpreters, lip speakers, advocates) who should be trained in equal opportunity interviews and disability equality (Stevens 1991). Since evidence suggests that interviewers tend to highlight problems (Walker 1995), disability awareness training and equal opportunity interviewing training should be provided for them. Disabled candidates should be assessed on their ability to complete the course successfully. Assumptions should not be made about a disabled person's needs and capabilities.

Disabled applicants who are to be offered a place should be involved in discussions about their special needs, and given the opportunity to visit the different facilities on which they might wish to draw, *before* arrival on the programme. An agreement should be reached as to the resources which the programme and institution will provide. This should be recorded to avoid subsequent disputes (Skidmore 1995). The agreement should be monitored regularly and, where necessary, revised. Once again, due process indicates the importance of the presence of a McKenzie friend (an advocate) (see paragraph 3:11), the right to be heard, and the right to reasons for any decision.

The admitting programme should contact members of staff within the institution, and grant-making authorities, *before* the student arrives on the programme to ensure that:

- applications are processed in advance of the student's arrival to minimise any delays in accessing resources once a claim is accepted;
- the necessary support, technical services, recognition of needs, and access to specialist resources are available.

Skidmore (1995) has drawn attention to instances where disabled students have been accepted onto programmes but where promised support has not materialised. Programmes must be able to deliver what is required to enable students to complete the programme of study.

Applicants are not legally required to provide information at interview about a disability, but they have a duty under section 7, Health and Safety at Work Act 1974, once on the programme, to disclose a disability if it affects safety at work. If employees provide false information to employers about a disability, and if they are dismissed as a result, whether this is fair will depend on whether it is reasonable in the circumstances of the case (RADAR 1992). This would need to be established by the nature of the work, the effect of the disability on it, and whether an employer could make reasonable adjustments to the work and/or working environment as set out in section 6 of the DDA 1995 (see paragraph 7:4). Training programmes could adopt similar procedures for occasions where a disability is acquired or becomes apparent during a programme of study. Once again, the importance of procedures is highlighted.

Some academic institutions have a nominated officer who provides the support referred to in paragraphs 13:6 and 13:7. Commonly they co-ordinate any assessments which might be necessary, for instance of dyslexia; ensure that all the available grants are applied for; and monitor accessibility to buildings. Social work programmes should have a member of staff with responsibility for liaison with the nominated officer before the student's admission to the programme. Thereafter tutors will be responsible for ensuring that curriculum delivery and assessment procedures respond appropriately to the needs of disabled students. Accordingly, tutors must have the necessary understanding of issues faced by disabled students which could form part of an ongoing training focus. Finally, procedures should be monitored, including asking disabled students for feedback on what more needs to be done to ensure their progression.

Chapter 14
Language and training:
from entry to qualification

The Welsh Language Act 1993 gives a mandate for Welsh language provision. The right to choose a language for interaction becomes, then, both a legal principle and good practice. Bilingual people may feel better able to express themselves and to demonstrate their ability in their chosen language (E. Davies, 1994). However, choice may be determined by the nature and context of the discussion to take place, and by personal and organisational factors such as issues of power, vulnerability, confidence, institutional validation of choice, and self-esteem. In such situations trainers need to demonstrate the anti-discriminatory practice skills that they require of students, in order to ensure genuine choice based on a sharing and transfer of power.

Recruitment publicity should be available in Welsh. Where candidates so choose, interviews should be conducted in the medium of Welsh. Similarly, training institutions should include in their Welsh language schemes (see chapter 10) how they intend to provide their programme in the medium of Welsh. This will probably include provision:
● for professional translation of essays and student verification that the translation is fair;
● of timetabled language tuition courses;
● of placements, assessment and teaching in the medium of Welsh, and a choice where possible of a Welsh speaking tutor.

Collins *et al.* (1997) also refer to the provision of simultaneous translation at meetings and lectures, bilingual written documents and teaching materials, and annual monitoring which includes students' views. Programmes are likely also to include inputs on language issues, the outline content of which is likely to be highly pertinent as a basis for teaching in programmes outside Wales.

In spite of the multi-cultural composition of society, there is no comparable mandate in relation to other languages. However, it is recognised that S/NVQ assessment need not necessarily be in English. Thus, in Northern Ireland S/NVQ assessment may be undertaken in Irish providing the work undertaken by the candidate is through the medium of Irish. External verifiers do not need to read or speak Irish; rather the assessment centre is responsible for providing a translator (Patricia Higgins, personal communication, May 1996). Elsewhere, S/NVQ assessment may be conducted in a variety of different spoken and sign languages where the competence being assessed is not written or spoken English; and where verifiers, assessors and candidates can communicate directly or through an interpreter in the language chosen by the candidate. Students are more likely to feel empowered if they are encouraged to use the language in which they usually express themselves.

The importance of professional translators and interpreters is illustrated by the difference between ordinary language and professional language. As the CRE cautions (1992), it is inappropriate to rely on bilingual staff because language ability does not necessarily mean skills in translation and interpretation, including knowledge of terms, and the specific meaning and nuances of everyday words in professional practice. The employment of professional translators and interpreters needs also to be accompanied by staff training to ensure their most effective use, and the provision of literature and signs in the most commonly used languages. A useful illustration of these points occurred during the preparation of this book. The professional translator translated a phrase into English as 'revealing interviews' when what was under discussion were 'disclosure interviews' involving police officers, social workers and young people giving evidence about abuse which they had experienced.

DipSW programmes are not, generally speaking, as advanced as S/NVQ assessment procedures in relation to language. Clearly, where the competence and skills to be assessed include written or spoken English, that should be the medium of assessment, although the provision of language tuition courses would be appropriate where students indicate such a learning need. However, when the competences to be assessed include skills in working with people from minority groups, critical reflection and critical analysis, a choice of the language medium for presentation ought to be provided. The level of proficiency, or standard of competence required, of written or spoken English should be justifiable and only to the level necessary to perform the work which is the subject of the assessment. The level of proficiency should be detailed in programme documentation.

Language is often at the root of oppression and discrimination (E. Davies, 1994). The language in which the S/NVQ units and DipSW requirements are written should not exclude people because it is unclear and ambiguous, or inappropriate. Monitoring of the language used, and the assumptions this betrays, should form part of programme and assessment centre activity.

Chapter 15
Academic curriculum delivery and assessment

Joining a programme of study is a challenging moment. Accordingly, induction is critically important for new students, introducing them to a new environment and preparing them as fully as possible for the demands and experiences of qualifying training. Clearly, it is important to focus on "task", reminding students of information given at the entry or selection point; setting out programme requirements and regulations; ensuring that the programme's policies are clearly known, and that there is an awareness of what is expected, both generally and in relation to assignments. However, it is equally important to concentrate on "process" issues. Students not uncommonly experience varying levels of bewilderment, feeling deskilled, and ill-at-ease. They may transfer previous experiences, whether or not of education and training, and anticipate either opportunity or difficulty. They may bring a sense of failure which leads them to doubt their ability and to question the "wisdom" of those who selected them (Aymer and Bryan 1996). Yet others may find the experience of being involved and consulted, of being encouraged to voice their concerns, experiences and issues unfamiliar, to which they may react with excitement or scepticism. Induction is the opportunity to set the tone for the remainder of the programme, to demonstrate that anti-discriminatory practice and equal opportunity can be realised through management of process and the dynamics which arise in programme delivery and, particularly, through the validation of experience, comment and difference.

Evidence emerges regularly of discriminatory features in programme delivery. Research by Campbell (1995) into student experiences found that younger students felt that they were not taken seriously because assumptions based on age appeared to discount ability and achievement. Course content and teaching material was criticised for inadequate acknowledgement of lesbian and gay issues and experiences, and for the presence of sexist assumptions (Trotter and Gilchrist 1996, report similar findings). Students from a working class background felt disadvantaged by the language and curriculum material used. Some students requested that black and feminist perspectives should become more central in the curriculum, and that staff should challenge more actively sexist, heterosexist and racist assumptions and behaviour as it occurred in teaching sessions.

Coulson (1993) found that curriculum development was slow or uneven, and that there was a need for staff to re-evaluate their tutorial practice. Black students (see, for example, Burgess *et al.* 1992) reported concerns about the quality, quantity and content of antiracist and black perspectives within the academic curriculum, and rightly suggest that all subjects should carry a black dimension. Thus, teaching materials, resource packs, reading lists, and guidelines for essays should validate different perspectives. Students should not be marked down for using their own (say) black perspectives.

Because of manager/worker relationships, difficulties can arise within S/NVQ assessment around race, gender and power (see, for example, Burton *et al.* 1992). The NVQ 0 Unit, on promoting equality for all individuals, is not always fully integrated into other units, including D units which provide training for verifiers and assessors. As with DipSW programmes, how to permeate teaching materials and learning opportunities with anti-discriminatory practice is a major concern. Bias within assessment may arise because of institutional racism, for instance. Competences may be culturally inappropriate for black service users, while black candidates may not be put forward for training (Ferns 1992; Stokes 1996). The competence approach within S/NVQ and DipSW aims to promote equal opportunities but assessment of competence may be affected by issues of race and gender. It is not value-free, independent of its social and organisational context (Kemshall 1993).

Black, disabled, gay and lesbian students are reported to feel isolated irrespective of their numbers within the overall course membership. Similarly, students from minority groups may be asked to be the programme's "experts". Courses are not necessarily supportive of them. Equally, given that assessment is rooted in the values of the organisation, and that within institutions white, male values predominate, students from minority groups should be offered mentors to support and guide them (Burton *et al.* 1992; Kemshall 1993). Access to support networks, for example to students on other programmes, is important. Where consultants are provided, care should be taken not to assume that black or disabled students belong to homogeneous groups. Disabled students and gay and lesbian students should be given an opportunity to disclose their position and, with black students, be given the opportunity to be grouped together for groupwork, tutorials and seminars in order to reduce any sense of isolation and to provide an opportunity for mutual support. A peer-assisted support scheme, whereby second year students assist first year students, is also possible. Where programmes are geographically close, some co-operation should be possible. These opportunities should be an integral feature of programmes, and not facilities just to be provided when students experience difficulties (Burgess *et al.* 1992).

It is unlawful under sections 17 and 20 of the RRA 1976; 22 and 29 of the SDA 1975; 21-23 of the Fair Employment (NI) Act 1976, and 20 of the Fair Employment (NI) Act 1989 for an educational establishment to discriminate on grounds of race, sex and religion in the way education, or services and facilities are offered. Thus, in relation to curriculum delivery and assessment, direct discrimination would arise if a person was given a lower assessment because of assumptions about the ability and characteristics of (say) racial groups. Direct discrimination would arise if less favourable or biased comments and assessment were made because of a person's racial origins. Indirect discrimination (see paragraph 5:4) might result if assessment criteria or procedures, or curriculum material were culturally biased. Assumptions about the uniformity of perspective or linguistic experience would be an example of cultural bias, leading to a lower assessment of a higher proportion of students from a particular (say) racial group, as would curriculum material or criteria not being justified on educational grounds. The assessment criteria and support material may set down requirements or conditions for passing which, while apparently applied equally, lead to a smaller proportion of one particular group being likely to be able to comply.

For these reasons, for monitoring purposes and in the interests of greater openness, marking criteria and information on how direct observation is to be assessed should be published and checked for cultural and other bias, and for relevance to the subject being assessed. All students should be assessed on their understanding of a subject rather than the level of their oral or written skills, and tutors should comment in ways which facilitate their learning. Good practice includes anonymous marking, the provision of study skills tuition which encompasses reading scripts to provide feedback on the use of language, and the supply of guidance for managing issues of discrimination in relation to simulation exercises and seminar work.

Disabled students are legally in a weaker position as explained in paragraph 13:1. Walker (1995) has cited examples of good practice in curriculum delivery and assessment of disabled students. They include provision of tape machines to record lectures and seminars and to enable students to submit recorded assignments; videoing of lectures; facilities to produce Braille materials; and agreements on course work and assignments, which allow for specially devised or adapted methods and times of assessment. Importantly, a range of assessment methods should be used. Written work is only one indicator of conceptual ability and competence. Good practice requires discussion with disabled students as to whether special assistance or expert consultation is necessary, together with a specific induction programme.

However, studies still indicate an emphasis on written work which disadvantages some disabled students (Campbell 1995), and record a failure to provide promised notetakers, signers, adapted materials, and sub-titled videos. Disabled students may fear joining a programme. They may find that staff have little awareness of disability issues, that they are treated as clients rather than students, that inappropriate remarks are made on their assignments, and that buildings provide inappropriate access, acoustics, lighting and colour (Campbell 1995; Taylor 1996).

For dyslexic students, a specialist assessment should be completed where one has not already been undertaken under section 4 of the Disabled Persons Act 1986 and section 165 of the Education Act 1993 (now incorporated as section 321 of the Education Act 1996). This assessment should feed into discussions concerning the appropriate formats and timing of assignments, and appropriate tutorial assistance and feedback while students are working on material. Assessors should inform themselves about a dyslexic student's level of written language understanding and presentation, and about the level and type of correction a student is able to use. Feedback that does not make sense for dyslexic students, as when assessors focus on spelling and grammar rather than on thinking patterns beyond this and on the material and use of ideas, may demoralise them.

External assessors and verifiers should be fully informed of disability issues in general (Stevens 1991) and may, of course, track specific students when their standard of work indicates that this is necessary.

The legislative mandates outlined in this chapter, together with the research findings, suggest that programmes should regularly undertake an audit of their curriculum structures, materials and assessment procedures. This audit should include a review of bibliographies and of assessment tasks in order to eliminate disadvantage and bias. It should scrutinise the images, writers, assumptions and perspectives included and omitted – for example, black perspectives, lesbian and gay issues – and comment upon the breadth of literature drawn on. Booklists should include material drawn from outside social work. The format of materials would be reviewed and, for disabled students especially, the time when they were made available. The audit would monitor marking, for instance with reference to markers' understanding and validation of black perspectives. It would monitor students' performance in particular modules or units and overall completion rates, enquiring into situations where overall failure rates are high or where students from particular groups appear over-represented in failure and non completion statistics. Students should be involved in this process. Audits should be both planned and unannounced. Materials should be updated and revised to incorporate new knowledge and research. Assessment criteria should be evaluated, to monitor for prejudice, bias and partiality (Kemshall 1993), and to ensure that all anti-discriminatory issues are covered, including those surrounding heterosexism and homophobia (Trotter and Gilchrist 1996).

If students withdraw before completing the course, exit interviews should be held to discuss the reasons for the decision and what the programme may learn from it.

Key questions for programme providers, therefore, include (CRE/EOC 1995):
- how do programmes take account of different people's experiences, expectations and concerns?
- how do courses seek to create a learning environment free from discrimination?
- how are achievement levels monitored for ethnic group and gender, and how are the results of monitoring used to inform policy and practice?
- what training and guidance do staff receive to help them distinguish between language needs and difficulties arising from learning difficulties, and to assist them in providing appropriate

support?
- is a range of assessment methods used in order to do justice to people's different aptitudes?
- is there a mechanism for reviewing the work of assessors and for rectifying any unjustified disparities?

Chapter 16
The practice curriculum

The legislative mandate outlawing discrimination in race, gender and religion described in chapter 15 applies also to practice placements for students. Educational institutions must not discriminate in the provision of educational services and facilities (see paragraphs 5:13 and 6:1 and also sections 17 and 20 of the RRA 1976; 22 and 29 of the SDA 1975; 21-23 of the Fair Employment (NI) Act 1976, and 20 of the Fair Employment (NI) Act 1989). Thus, for example, it would be unlawful to allocate placements on racial grounds. However, some placements are located in organisations which provide services for a particular racial group or gender, such as a black women's refuge, and where a genuine occupational qualification would be used in job advertisements (see paragraph 5:10). The genuine occupational qualification exemptions are not, however, applicable to students. Programmes and placement providers should, therefore, by way of a code of good practice devise a person specification and job description which identify the learning opportunities and training available, and the reasons why the educational purpose of the placement indicates a student of a particular gender or racial group. The person specification may be based on the provision of personal services designed to promote a person's welfare and where that provision can most effectively and appropriately be provided by a person of a particular racial group or gender. Placements should be considered *individually* in this regard. In relation to services to meet the special training needs of particular racial groups, section 35 of the RRA 1976 may be useful (see paragraph 6:5). Each placement should be looked at *individually* in order to establish whether the special training needs of students from a particular racial group justify provision relying on section 35.

Helpfully too a limited number of legal cases relate to placements. It has been held to be unlawful under section 31 of the RRA 1976 for an employer or organisation to put pressure on an educational institution not to place students from a racial group and for the educational institution to give in to such pressure (CRE *v Fearn and British Electrical Repairs Ltd* [1987]). Similarly, again under section 31, a social services department could be acting illegally if it replaced a black student with a white student because of a refusal by a service user to work with the former (CRE *v Roper* [1987]). However, it would clearly be unacceptable to override, or be unresponsive towards the feelings of the worker in such instances. Similarly, placing a black student in a racist area could constitute discrimination if the placement provider and programme failed to take reasonable steps to discuss the allocation with the student, and to prevent or reduce the extent of any harassment through good employment and training practice (see paragraphs 17.3 and 17.9). This includes pressure placed on the student to accept such an allocation, even if because of a shortage of placements.

However, black students continue to voice concern about unfair allocation of placements, and about racism in practice placements as contributing to placement breakdown or failure (Burgess *et al.* 1992; Coulson 1993). Women students also report concern about allocation, particularly from the perspective of personal safety and caring commitments (Campbell 1995).

Good practice would indicate, when implementing the legislative mandate referred to above, that programmes:
- have clear procedures for placement allocation, and a system for hearing representations and complaints;
- have clear procedures to be followed when a student refuses to accept a placement;
- monitor placements, involving students and programme (agency and college) staff, for their approach to counteracting discrimination;
- contract with placement providers to include specifications relating to anti-discriminatory practice with students and within the learning opportunities provided;
- ensure that contracts between students and practice teachers include details about the management of power in supervision, the agency's policies on counteracting discrimination and delivering equal opportunities for staff and service users, and the location of support for students/employees;
- have clear procedures to minimise disadvantage arising from difficulties in providing placements on time;
- have clear expectations, negotiated with placement providers, on hours of work and procedures in the event of illness, together with clarity on the support structures available to students, particularly those with caring responsibilities or from minority groups.

Disabled students have reported that agencies have not understood their placement needs or disability issues (Taylor 1996), and that disability has not been properly taken into account in placement negotiations (Campbell 1995). In his survey of opportunities for disabled students to qualify as social workers, Walker (1995) reported problems in obtaining suitable placements.

Paragraphs 13:1 and 15:8 suggested that the responsibilities of employers to disabled employees should be translated by programmes of study to the sphere of education and training. In relation to practice placements, this would have several implications. Disabled students would be expected to inform agencies of disabilities which would have implications for health and safety at work (see paragraph 13:8). Programmes should ensure that as wide a choice of training opportunities are offered to disabled students as to non-disabled students. Placement agencies should ensure that suitable arrangements are made in discussion with disabled students. If a disability became apparent, or was acquired during a placement, the agency and programme of study would be expected to give extra consideration to the student's needs, for instance in relation to time off. RADAR (1992) lists a number of employment cases, predating the Disability Discrimination Act 1995, which give helpful guidance both on how that Act might be interpreted by industrial tribunals, and on what employers should do to meet the needs of disabled staff. Agencies should take all reasonable steps to ensure that the working environment does not prevent disabled people from taking up placements or positions for which they are qualified (EL(95)143).

For the purposes of this chapter, agencies and programmes should, as good practice:
- not terminate a placement unless a student is incapable of performing a significant proportion of the job;
- take a medical condition fully into account when considering a student's behaviour at work, and focus not on whether an incident justifies termination of a placement but on whether the student is fit to return to work and capable of performing a significant proportion of the job;
- where practicable, adjust the nature of the placement or working conditions, to enable the student to continue.

Agencies should specify how they are responding to ensuring the accessibility of their facilities – what reasonable adjustments are they making to facilitate placement provision alongside employment of staff (see paragraph 7:3)? Since, arguably, practice teaching is a service, paragraph 7:5 also applies.

Once again, good practice would include:
- provision of support groups, with resources allocated by the

placement agency, for disabled workers to follow a planned programme;

● monitoring of placements, for instance for accessibility, and more widely, the implementation by placement providers of the DDA 1995;

● training on disability issues for practice teachers;

● contracts with programme providers to include specifications concerning equal opportunities and anti-discriminatory practice;

● contracts between students and practice teachers to include details about agency support for the student;

● a range of assessment methods appropriate for the student, including interpreters and translators where necessary.

Gay and lesbian students have queried the criteria for placement selection and safety, and the lack of sensitivity to risks deriving from institutional heterosexism and sexual politics which can reinforce unequal opportunities for them (Campbell 1995; Trotter and Gilchrist 1996). They recommend that placements be monitored for anti-discriminatory practice. For example, do their equal opportunity policies include sexuality? To develop awareness in this area, they recommend training and support for practice teachers and tutors.

No UK-wide legislation prevents discrimination on grounds of sexuality in employment, subject to the caveats that sex discrimination may arise if different criteria are applied to men than women in interviews (paragraph 11:9), and that discrimination on grounds of sexuality may be contrary to the European Union's Equal Treatment Directive (see paragraphs 2:8-2:10). The picture is scarcely better in the area of service provision. In relation to criminal justice, the publication of information might encourage those involved in provision not to discriminate against any person on grounds of race, sex or any other improper ground as prescribed in section 95 of the Criminal Justice Act 1991, but this applies to England and Wales only. Nor is there a duty not to discriminate in the Act. The welfare of children in need and of children and young people looked after by local authorities should be paramount in providing services for them. Thus, while guidance does not disqualify gay and lesbian people from adoption and foster care (DH 1991), social services departments and welfare agencies are not prohibited from setting policies which discriminate in service provision against gay and lesbian people, providing they can demonstrate that they fall within the requirements just identified. Programmes of study will have to decide for themselves their response to agencies which do not include within their equal opportunities policies anti-discriminatory statements concerning sexuality.

The principles outlined in paragraph 15:6 apply to the practice curriculum. In relation to curriculum delivery and assessment, discrimination is unlawful. Thus, some S/NVQ assessment centres have ensured that assessors make themselves available during night shifts to open up appropriate awards to night staff, or have authorised child care payments to enable part-time workers to attend courses.

The procedures in respect of students who are failing placement should be clearly specified in a handbook. The Second Opinion Practice Teacher, when appointed to consider the evidence and to interview practice teachers, students and tutors in such cases, should reflect the race and gender of the student. The Practice Assessment Panel, responsible for monitoring the standards of placement reports and for the quality of placement provision, should publish guidelines for anti-discriminatory practice and for report writing. The grounds for appeal should be published, namely that regulations and procedures have not been followed, and/or that information was not available to the Programme Assessment Board which might have influenced the final decision. Appeals procedures should be given to each student and due process (see chapter 3) followed.

The requirements of anti-discriminatory practice appear daunting to practice teachers (Balen *et al.* 1993). Support groups in agencies, for instance for black practice teachers/staff, and for gay and lesbian practice teachers/staff, with a training and support programme annually negotiated, are recommended. Training for assessors and for practice teachers should form part of an organisation's training policy which annually identifies and monitors people's developmental needs through supervision, consultation and appraisal.

Placement finding can create considerable anxiety for students and programmes alike, principally because of shortages. Providers should not offer places on a programme unless they are confident that placements can be provided (see paragraph 12:2), should not promise to secure *specific* placements, and must make reasonable efforts to find placements appropriate to a student's learning needs within an appropriate timescale (Skidmore 1993). Otherwise students may have a remedy through the courts.

Chapter 17
Harassment

Racial, sexual or disability harassment, while not specifically referred to in the legislation, constitute racial, sexual or disability discrimination. Harassment is unlawful, therefore, in employment, education, and in the provision of facilities or services. It includes physical assault, verbal abuse and any other form of behaviour perceived as humiliating, offensive or distressing, intimidating or demeaning. Harassment constitutes less favourable treatment and is unlawful. Sexual harassment in the work place is also contrary to the European Community's Equal Treatment Directive.

Harassment is a detriment if the person experiences humiliation, anger as a result of offensive remarks or behaviour, or is disadvantaged in employment (*De Souza v Automobile Association* [1986]; *Porcelli v Strathclyde Regional Council* [1986]). An employer may be liable for the actions of an employee unless it can be shown that the employer has taken reasonable steps to prevent discrimination (see paragraph 2:4 and chapter 5). In this instance, a policy which defines what harassment is, outlines the procedure to be followed, and provides training for those responsible for its implementation, might satisfy an industrial tribunal. Clearly, students should be informed of the policies and procedures which agencies have for counteracting harassment.

Similarly, an employer may be liable when they *subject* an employee to the detriment of racial and sexual harassment; that is, if they cause or permit harassment serious enough to amount to a detriment in circumstances in which they can control whether it happens or not (*Burton and Rhule v De Vere Hotels* [1996]). Foresight of events, or the lack of it, does not determine whether the events were under the employer's control. Where the harasser is a third party and not in the employment of the employers, the question will turn on whether the event was something sufficiently under the control of the employers that they could, by adopting good employment practice, have prevented it or reduced its extent. The implications of this case are potentially far reaching. Those involved in the provision of education and training will need to ensure, so far as is reasonably practicable, that where they are "in control" harassment does not arise or, if it does arise, is appropriately dealt with, whether the "victim" of the harassment is an employee or a student, and whether the alleged "harasser" is an employee, student, or third party (Rachel Dineley, personal communication).

It follows that academic institutions, assessment centres and welfare organisations should have a policy and procedure, and should train staff to handle complaints and cases of harassment (EL(96)4). Equally, training should be provided for all staff to help them deal effectively with harassment from users of their service or from members of the public, and to ensure that they acquire an understanding of the likely effect of different types of behaviour. However, there has been a poor management response. Employers have been slow to introduce policies (Collier 1995) and staff may feel that access to procedures is effectively denied because of the potential effect on career prospects of complaining (Cockburn 1991).

One incident may be sufficient to prove harassment (*Bracebridge Engineering Company v Darby* [1990]). An employer may be liable for a finding of constructive dismissal if they did not take the matter seriously.

Racial and sexual harassment are not formally defined in law but may be taken to include deliberate isolation or non-co-operation, the display of offensive material, derogatory or unwelcome remarks, threats, abuse and assault (unwanted verbal or physical behaviour, with racial or sexual elements (Malone 1993)). Since the determining factor in sexual harassment is the gender of the recipient, all forms of harassment on grounds of the recipient's sex are unlawful whether of women by men, men by women, women by women, men by men. Although the DDA 1995 does not contain a specific section relating to harassment of disabled people, because harassment means less favourable treatment to the employee's detriment, this constitutes discrimination within the meaning of the Act (section 4) (Gooding, 1996).

To meet their obligations and to avoid potential liability, employers should (Collier 1995):
- have a written policy which states that harassment will not be condoned, that all complaints will be investigated and, where necessary, people disciplined;
- provide definitions and examples of harassment;
- allocate responsibility for investigating complaints and for monitoring the policy's effectiveness;
- provide training for all staff on the policy (for example, on the steps to take if they are the recipient) and for those responsible for

implementing it;
- communicate the policy to all staff;
- ensure that the procedure includes the right of appeal.

The goal is a clear procedure so that staff will know to whom to complain and how the complaint will be dealt with.

The procedure should include provision for an informed assessment of risk that the alleged abuser poses to the complainant, in order to decide about their continued participation at work (at all locations or in the same/different one), while the matter is investigated. It is essential that the investigation is carried out promptly and completed as quickly as possible. Any victimisation of the complainant arising from their use of the procedures, or of people giving evidence on their behalf, could constitute a further act of discrimination under the legislation, should constitute a disciplinary offence and, in relation to students, may result in them being asked to leave the course, using the provisions for unsuitable students (Skidmore, 1993). Victims should be offered post-incident support and/or counselling.

Black employees and students may find that service users refuse to work with them, demonstrate racist attitudes and engage in racist behaviour. An employer may be guilty of discriminating against a black employee or student if the latter suffered detriment as a result of the employer's failure to respond to the service user's behaviour (*Jeffers v North Wales Probation Committee* [1995]; *Burton and Rhule v De Vere Hotels* [1996]). Invitations to employers by service users to discriminate by refusing to allocate a black worker are outlawed by sections 30 and 31 of the RRA 1976, and so should be immediately rejected. Failure to do so represents a failure to provide the support to which, as a professional, the worker is entitled to expect from an employer.

Part 4

Implications and further reading

ACEGENDERLANGUAGE
ISABILITYEQUALOPPOR
UNITIESSEXUALITYLAW
UIDANCEPRACTICERACE
ENDERLANGUAGEDISA
ILITYEQUALOPPORTUN
IESSEXUALITYLAWGUID

Chapter 18
Implications for programme providers

There are four implications for practice derived from the legislative mandate and codes of practice which will be highlighted in this chapter:

1 Equal opportunities policies
2 Training
3 Monitoring
4 Redress

1. Equal opportunities policies

Paragraph 2:4 indicated that an equal opportunity policy could be taken as indicative of an organisation's attempt to take reasonable and practicable steps to prevent acts of discrimination. Such policies will need to address the legislative mandate but should be broadened to cover areas where the law is silent. An example here would be sectarianism outside Northern Ireland. DipSW programme providers, and NVQ training and assessment centres should, therefore, require that partner or constituent agencies have appropriate equal opportunity and anti-discriminatory policies. Guidance on the construction of policies was given in paragraph 3:14.

To reiterate, an equal opportunity policy should:
● identify the legal position;
● state objectives;
● identify people's roles in implementing the policy, both those with specific responsibilities and everyone's general duties;
● identify the types of good practice which the policy seeks to encourage;
● cover the administration of all aspects of a training programme, from recruitment through to assessment;
● include provisions for monitoring and review.

2. Training

Practice teachers and tutors not uncommonly feel uncertain about equal opportunity interviewing and how to give proper regard to anti-discriminatory practice when recruiting, selecting and giving access to training opportunities. They are also concerned about how to assess anti-discriminatory practice in the academic and practice curricula. Training should therefore be provided on these aspects if institutions are to be seen to be taking steps to prevent discrimination in the assessment of competence. Both the CRE (1984) and EOC (1985) codes of practice on employment emphasise that training is an essential part of an organisation's practicable and reasonable steps to prevent discrimination. For the effective implementation of anti-discriminatory practice, training is vital. A training strategy should aim to increase people's understanding of the law, equal opportunities, and how discrimination can arise. It should aim to increase their knowledge of issues connected with race, gender, disability and sexuality, both generally and in relation to their impact on the provision of education and training.

18:4

Training should involve *all* members of staff, from receptionists to senior managers. Training providers should involve disabled people and people from minority groups appropriately. Service users can also present a valuable perspective. The training should be ongoing and cover all aspects of programme provision, from recruitment, through assessment, to the management of complaints procedures.

3. Monitoring

18:5

The CRE (1984) and EOC (1985) codes of practice also recommend monitoring of all aspects of employment. All aspects of programme provision should be monitored, from recruitment and selection (who applies, with what outcomes; who is selected), through assessment (outcomes for students), to comments on the adequacy and quality of provision. Students and others involved with the programme should be included in the process of identifying the questions which monitoring will seek to address, and the methodology to be used. The approach should enable hypotheses about the differential impact on students of the programme's approach to be tested and recommendations for procedural and practice change backed up by evidence to be made.

4. Redress

18:6

This guide has emphasised the importance of administrative competence. The CRE, EOC and FEC have the power to investigate an organisation, to issue non-discrimination notices concerning specified provisions in the Acts which established them, and to require organisations to take steps to avoid discrimination in future. Legal proceedings can be initiated if organisations persist in unlawful discrimination.

Individuals also have the power to seek redress: in industrial tribunals for employment cases, and the county courts (sheriff courts in Scotland) for non-employment cases. The DDA 1995 follows the same format. In matters relating to education and training, sections 19 of the RRA 1976 and 25 of the SDA 1975 require a matter to be referred first to the Secretary of State for possible action.

Whether the procedures relate to complaints, recruitment and selection, appeals procedures under assessment regulations, or procedures to investigate concerns that a student may not be suitable to hold a professional qualification, they must be administratively sound, fair, and conducted without bias. They must consider all the facts available, and the decisions reached must be reasonable, communicated in writing, and supported by clear reasons (see chapter 3).

Given that there should be clear responsibility for an overview of equal opportunities issues, where should this be located? Whether there is a specialist sub-committee which monitors performance, and/or whether equal opportunities is an item for all main committees and panels responsible for the operation of a training programme or assessment centre, the maintenance of change requires a strong enough infrastructure.

This infrastructure must include:
● allocating authority to seek information and to act on the findings;
● monitoring all policies and actions for their impact on equal opportunities and for inbuilt assumptions;
● recognising imbalances of power and empowering people to ask questions and to challenge;
● creating an organisational culture which is open to (un)learning and to involving everyone (staff, students, community groups, local offices of the CRE and EOC) in determining how the goals of equality and organisational change are to be defined and pursued;
● locating overall co-ordination of development and monitoring.

Assessment centres, programme providers, and organisations providing health and welfare services are often part of larger organisations. The management of these organisations should:
● demonstrate their commitment to equal opportunities (CRE/EOC 1995) in the composition and activities of their governing bodies

or key committees;
- practise the values informing their aims and objectives;
- allocate responsibility for implementing, communicating and monitoring equal opportunities policies; and
- adequately resource training and recruitment procedures.

Conclusion

18:11

In keeping with social work's commitment to equal opportunities and anti-discriminatory practice, those involved in all sectors of education and training must engage with issues of injustice and discrimination. This guide has provided details about the legislative mandate which underpins this commitment, the codes of practice which illuminate how the legal mandate should be interpreted, and the implications for practice.

18:12

The law is not a complete mandate for anti-discriminatory practice and equal opportunities, and even equal opportunity policies and procedures which are more broadly drawn will not redress inequality alone (Smyth and Campbell 1996). Much, ultimately, depends on the commitment of individuals and organisations to recognise inequality in education and training, to listen, to express curiosity and scrutinise their own and other people's practice, and to offer constructive feedback and challenge. This will require skills in challenging resistance, giving meaning to values and principles, developing and assessing policies and practices, and managing organisational change. These are the very skills of social work.

RACEGENDERLANGUA
GEDISABILITYEQUALO
PPORTUNITIESSEXUAL
TYLAWGUIDANCEPRA
CTICERACEGENDERLA
NGUAGEDISABILITYEQ
UALOPPORTUNITIESSE
XUALITYLAWGUIDAN
CEPRACTICERACEGEN
DERLANGUAGEDISABI
LITYEQUALOPPORTUN

Useful addresses

Commission for Racial Equality
10-12 Allington Street, London SW1E 5EH

Commission for Racial Equality for Northern Ireland
Scottish Legal House, 65-67 Chichester Street, Belfast BT1 4JT

Employment Service
Disability Services Branch, Courtwood House, Silver Street Head
Sheffield Sl 2DD

Equal Opportunities Commission
Overseas House, Quay Street, Manchester M3 3HN

Equal Opportunities Commission for Northern Ireland
Chamber of Commerce House, Great Victoria Street, Belfast BT2

Fair Employment Commission
Andras House, 60 Great Victoria Street, Belfast BT2 7BB

Royal Association for Disability and Rehabilitation (RADAR)
12 City Forum, 250 City Road, London EC1V 8AF

Further reading

References

Aymer, C. and Bryan, A. (1996) 'Black students' experiences on social work courses: accentuating the positives' in *British Journal of Social Work* Vol. 26(1), pp.1-16

Balen, R., Brown, K. and Taylor, C. (1993) '"It seems that so much is expected of us": practice teachers, the Diploma in Social Work and anti-discriminatory practice' in *Social Work Education* Vol. 12(3), pp.17-40

Ball, C., Preston-Shoot, M., Roberts, G. and Vernon, S. (1995) *Law for Social Workers in England and Wales* London: CCETSW

Banton, M. (1994) *Discrimination* Buckingham: Open University Press

British Association of Social Workers (1989) *Rights, Responsibilities and Remedies: BASW's Model Complaints Procedure* Birmingham: BASW

Bond, H. (1996) 'Positively speaking' in *Community Care* 6-12 June, page 21

Booth, T., Bilson, A. and Fowell, I. (1990) 'Staff attitudes and caring practices in homes for the elderly' in *British Journal of Social Work* Vol. 20(2), pp.117-131

Buckley, J., Preston-Shoot, M. and Smith, C. (1995) *Community Care Reforms: The Views of Users and Carers* University of Manchester School of Social Work

Burgess, R., Crosskill, D. and LaRose-Jones, L. (1992) *The Black Students' Voice* London: Association of Black Probation Officers/Association of Black Social Workers and Allied Professions/CCETSW

Burton, S., Dutt, R. and Lyn-Cook, S. (eds) (1992) *Black Perspectives in National Vocational Qualifications* London: Race Equality Unit

Butt, J., Gorbach, P. and Ahmad, B. (1991) *Equally Fair? A Report on Social Services Departments' Development, Implementation and Monitoring of Services for the Black and Minority Ethnic Community* London: Race Equality Unit, National Institute for Social Work

Campbell, J. (1995) *Discriminatory/Anti-discriminatory Practice in the West of Scotland Consortium Diploma in Social Work Programme: A Survey of Experience among Students* Glasgow: University of Strathclyde Department of Social Work

CCETSW (1994) *Guidelines for the Implementation of CCETSW's Welsh Language Policy* Cardiff: CCETSW Cymru

CCETSW (second revision, 1996) *Assuring Quality in the Diploma in Social Work – 1. Rules and Requirements for the DipSW* London: CCETSW

Clarke, L. (1994) *Discrimination* London: Institute of Personnel Management

Cockburn, C. (1991) *In the Way Of Women: Men's Resistance to Sex Equality in Organisations* London: Macmillan

Collier, R. (1995) *Combating Sexual Harassment in the Workplace* Buckingham: Open University Press

Collins, S., James, A., Lynn, E. and Williams, C. (1997) 'Welsh language developments on a social work course: the Bangor case' in *Social Work Education* Vol. 16(1), pp. 80-100

Coulson, M. (1993) *Catalysts or Victims of Change? The Pattern of Student Failure on Social Work Courses* London: CCETSW

Commission for Racial Equality (1984) *Race Relations Code of Practice for the Elimination of Racial Discrimination and the Promotion of Equality of Opportunity in Employment* London: CRE

Commission for Racial Equality (1985) *Positive Action and Equal Opportunity in Employment* London: CRE

Commission for Racial Equality (1992) *Race Relations Code of Practice in Primary Health Care Services* London: CRE

Commission for Racial Equality/Equal Opportunities Commission (1995) *Further Education and Quality: A Manager's Manual* London: CRE

Cooper, J. and Vernon, S. (1996) *Disability and the Law* London: Jessica Kingsley

Davies, E. (1994) *'They All Speak English Anyway' – The Welsh Language and Anti-Oppressive Practice* Cardiff: CCETSW Cymru

Davies, G.P. (1994) 'The Welsh language and legislation', in Williams, R.H., Williams, H. and Davies, E. (eds) *Social Work and the Welsh Language* Cardiff: University of Wales Press

Department of Employment Group (1984) *Code of Good Practice on the Employment of Disabled People* Sheffield: DEG, Disability Services Branch

de Gale, H. (1991) 'Black students' views of existing CQSW courses and CSS schemes: 2', in Northern Curriculum Development Project *Setting the Context for Change* CCETSW

de Souza, P. (1991) 'A review of the experiences of black students in social work training' in CCETSW *One Small Step Towards Racial Justice* London: CCETSW

Dean, H. and Hartley, G. (1995) 'Listen to Learn' in *Community Care* 30 March-5 April

Department of Health and Social Services (Northern Ireland) (1989) *Disclosure of Criminal Background of Persons Seeking Access to Children or Mentally Handicapped People* Belfast: DHSS (NI)

Department of Health (1990) *Community Care In the Next Decade and Beyond: Policy Guidance* London: HMSO

Department of Health (1991) *The Children Act 1989 Guidance and Regulations, Volume 3. Family Placements* London: HMSO

Department of Health Social Services Inspectorate (1992) *Planning for Children and Young People: Writing Child Care Policy* London: DH

Department of Health Social Services Inspectorate (1993) *The Inspection of the Complaints Procedures in Local Authority Social Services Departments* London: DH

Dyer, C. (1993) 'Challenging state in court 'a lottery'' in *The Guardian* 21 June, page 4

Equal Opportunities Commission (1985) *Equal Opportunities Commission Code Of Practice: Equal Opportunity Policies, Procedures and Practices in Employment* London: HMSO

Equal Opportunities Commission (1988) *Guidelines for the Avoidance of Discriminatory Questions at Interview* Manchester: EOC

Everitt, A., Hardiker, P., Littlewood, J. and Mullender, A. (1992) *Applied Research for Better Practice* London: Macmillan

Ferns, P. (1992) 'Implications of S/NVQ for black people' in Burton, S., Dutt, R. and Lyn-Cook, S. (eds) *Black Perspectives in National Vocational Qualifications* London: Race Equality Unit, NISW

Gibson, F., Michael, G. and Wilson, D. (1994) *Perspectives on Discrimination and Social Work in Northern Ireland* Belfast: CCETSW

Gooding, C. (1996) *Disability Discrimination Act 1995* London: Blackstone Press

Guardian, The (1992) 'Long wait for equality' in *Education Guardian* 19 May, page 3

Home Office (1977) *Racial Discrimination. A Guide to the Race Relations Act 1976* London: HMSO

James, P. and Thomas, M. (1996) 'Deconstructing a disabling environment in social work education' in *Social Work Education* Vol. 15(1), pp. 34-45

Kemshall, H. (1993) 'Assessing competence: scientific process or subjective inference? Do we really see it?' in *Social Work Education* Vol. 12(1), pp. 36-45

Logan, J. and Kershaw, S. (1994) 'Heterosexism and social work education: the invisible challenge' in *Social Work Education* Vol. 13(3), pp. 61-80

Mallinson, I. and Best, E. (1990) 'Promoting power' in *Social Work Today* 29 March, pp. 24-25

Malone, M. (1993) *Discrimination Law. A Practical Guide for Management* London: Kogan Page

National Disability Council (1996a) *Disability Discrimination Act 1995 Code of Practice. Rights of Access: Goods, Facilities, Services and Premises* London: HMSO

National Disability Council (1996b) *Code of Practice for the Elimination of Discrimination in the Field of Employment against Disabled Persons or Persons who have had a Disability* London: HMSO

Phillipson, J. (1992) *Practising Equality: Women, Men and Social Work* London: CCETSW

Pink, D. (1991) 'Black students' views of existing CQSW courses and CSS schemes: 1' in Northern Curriculum Development Project *Setting the Context for Change* London: CCETSW

Preston-Shoot, M. (1996) 'Contesting the contradictions: needs, resources and community care decisions' in *Journal of Social Welfare and Family Law*, 3, pp. 307-325

Royal Association for Disability and Rehabilitation (1992) *Employment Rights. A Guide for Disabled People* London: RADAR

Royal Association for Disability and Rehabilitation (1994) *Half Measures: RADAR's Response to the Consultation Document on Government Measures to Tackle Discrimination Against Disabled People* London: RADAR

Simons, K. (1992) 'Who counts?' in *Community Care Supplement* 26 March, pp. iv-v

Simons, K. (1995) *I'm Not Complaining But ... Complaints Procedures In Social Services* York: Joseph Rowntree Foundation

Skidmore, A. (1993) *Legal Matters Relating to CCETSW Programmes* London: CCETSW

Skidmore, A. (1995) *Complaints Procedures and other matters* Letter to Diploma in Social Work Programme Correspondents, 13 October. London: CCETSW

Smyth, M. and Campbell, J. (1996) 'Social work, sectarianism and anti-sectarian practice in Northern Ireland' in *British Journal of Social Work* Vol. 26(1), pp. 77-92

Stevens, A. (1991) *Disability Issues: Developing Anti-discriminatory Practice* London: CCETSW

Stokes, I. (1996) 'Black practice teachers: a review of some literature and its meaning for social work education and practice' in *Social Work Education* Vol. 15(2) pp. 5-20

Taylor, G. (1996) 'A sense of real achievement? The experience of deaf students in social work and youth and community work training' in *Social Work Education* Vol. 15(1), pp. 46-74

Taylor, L. (ed.) (1992) *Equal Opportunities in Practice: A Resources Pack for Organisational and Staff Development in Higher Education* Sheffield: Committee of Vice Chancellors and Principals Staff Development and Training Unit

Trotter, J. and Gilchrist, J. (1996) 'Assessing DipSW students: anti-discriminatory practice in relation to lesbian and gay issues' in *Social Work Education* Vol. 15(1), pp. 75-82

Walker, M. (1995) *Opportunities for Disabled People to Qualify for a Career in Social Work*

Leeds: CCETSW

Welsh Language Board (1996) *Welsh Language Schemes: Their Preparation and Approval in accordance with the Welsh Language Act 1993* Cardiff: WLB

Whitaker, D. and Archer, L. (1994) 'Partnership research and its contributions to learning and to team-building' in *Social Work Education* Vol. 13(3), pp. 39-60

Young, K. and Connelly, N. (1984) 'After the act: local authority policy reviews under the Race Relations Act 1976' in *Local Government Studies* Vol. 10(1), pp. 13-25

Useful books not cited in the references

Ahmad, W. and Atkin, R. (eds) (1996) *'Race' and Community Care* Buckingham: Open University Press

Braye, S. and Preston-Shoot, M. (1997) *Practising Social Work Law* London: Macmillan, second edition

Brophy, J. and Smart, C. (eds) (1985) *Women-in-Law* London: Routledge and Kegan Paul

Cheung-Judge, M-Y. and Henley, A. (1994) *Equality in Action: Introducing Equal Opportunities in Voluntary Organisations* London: NCVO Publications

Commission for Racial Equality (1991) *Lessons of the Law: A Casebook of Racial Discrimination in Education* London: CRE

Department of the Environment (1996) *Challenging Religious Discrimination: A Guide for Faith Communities and their Advisers* London: DoE

Edwards, S. (ed.) (1985) *Gender, Sex and the Law* London: Croom Helm

Farish, M., McPake, J., Powney, J. and Weiner, G. (1995) *Equal Opportunities in Colleges and Universities. Towards Better Practices* Buckingham: Society for Research into Higher Education and Open University Press

Kennedy, H. (1993) *Eve Was Framed: Women and British Justice* London: Vintage Books

Little, A. and Robbins, D. (1982) *'Loading the Law': A Study of Transmitted Deprivation, Ethnic Minorities and Affirmative Action* London: CRE

Poulter, S. (1990) *Asian Traditions and English Law* Stoke on Trent: Trentham Books

See also books published by CCETSW in the Northern Curriculum Development (CD) Project series *Antiracist Social Work Education*. For example, Humphries, B., Pankhania-Wimmer, H., Seale, A. and Stokes, I. (1993) *Improving Practice Teaching and Learning: A Training Manual* makes helpful suggestions for the development of antiracist policies, procedures and practice in relation to placement provision.

Useful journals

Critical Social Policy
Legal Action
Local Government Studies
New Community
Race and Class.

Useful law reports

Current Law
Industrial Relations Law Reports.

Antiracist Social Work Education Series of publications from CCETSW

This widely acclaimed series was produced as part of CCETSW's Curriculum Development Project. Each title is available separately or at a discount rate for the complete set, comprising the initial core text and six training manuals.

1. Setting the Context for Change
Naina Patel and others
Gives a comprehensive and critical analysis of the state of racism, antiracism and Black struggles, with a focus on social work and social work education in Britain.
1991   0 904488 79 9   193 pages

2. Improving Practice with Children and Families
David Gambe, Jenny Gomes, Vijay Kapur, Moira Rangel and Paul Stubbs
Includes the implementation of the Children Act 1989 in a discussion of child care issues.
1992   1 85719 006 8   102 pages

3. Improving Practice with Elders
Arshi Ahmad-Aziz, Alison Froggatt, Ian Richardson, Terri Whittaker and Tim Leung
Identifies key issues in the law, the organisational context and in assessment, decision making and counselling skills.
1992   0 904488 99 3   106 pages

4. Improving Mental Health Practice
Pam Clarke, Mary Harrison, Kamlesh Patel, Mani Shah, Mary Varley and Tunde Zack-Williams
Guidelines to develop and consolidate sound mental health practice and assess progress.
1993   1 85719 021 1   226 pages

5. Improving Practice with People with Learning Disabilities
Aktar Bano, Daryl Crosskill, Rafiq Patel, Lyndsay Rashman and Robina Shah
A clear, antiracist perspective for training in the field, this looks at the connection between race and underachievement in education.
1993   1 85719 049 1   96 pages

6. Improving Practice in the Criminal Justice System
Hamilton de Gale, Peter Hanlon, Michael Hubbard, Steve Morgan with David Denney
For practising and prospective probation officers and their tutors, this manual aims to provide the means to develop sound antiracist practice.
1993   1 85719 053 X   110 pages

7. Improving Practice Teaching and Learning
Beth Humphries, Harsa Pankhania-Wimmer, Alex Seale and Idris Stokes
Designed to help programme providers establish antiracist policies and practice in education and training.
1993   1 85719 032 7   96 pages

Other related publications from **CCETSW**

Law for Social Workers in England and Wales
Caroline Ball, Michael Preston-Shoot, Dr Gwyneth Roberts and Stuart Vernon
Guidance as it relates to England and Wales, including changes in substantive law and issues in the teaching of law on social work.
1995   1 85719 118 8   60 pages

Law for Social Workers in Scotland
Kathryn Cameron
Guidance as it relates to Scotland, including the Children (Scotland) Act 1995 and the criminal process in Scotland.
1996   1 85719 155 2   64 pages

Law for Social Workers in Northern Ireland
Ruth Lavery, Colette McAuley, Mary McColgan, Anne McKeown, Patricia Higgins
Guidance as it relates to Northern Ireland, including the implementation of the Children (NI) Order 1995 and the Children's Evidence (NI) Order.
1997   1 85719 164 1   80 pages

Education, Social Work and the Law
Sets out the aims of law teaching for social work settings in England and Wales and aims to help prepare social work students in the education aspects of work with children.
1995   1 85719 088 2   40 pages

Assuring Quality in the Diploma in Social Work – 1: Rules and Requirements for the DipSW
Describes the skills and abilities that DipSW students are required to demonstrate on qualifying and the rules and requirements that programme providers need to satisfy in their programmes.
1996   1 85719 168 4   52 pages (Welsh/English bilingual edition also available)

Back from the Wellhouse: discussion papers on sensory impairment and training in community care
Aims to help students of social work and other caring professions involved in care management begin to identify the methods by which they can learn to communicate with deaf, blind or other sensorily impaired service users on their own terms.
1993   1 85719 054 8   190 pages

Reflections: views of disabled people on their lives and community care
edited by Nasa Begum, Mildrette Hill and Andy Stevens
"We use this book" writes Nasa Begum, "to reflect on our lives and start a dialogue with those of you who have the power to support and empower other Black Disabled people either directly through social work practice, or indirectly through policy and practice formulation."
1994   1 85719 0815   200 pages

"They All Speak English Anyway"
Welsh/English bilingual training pack on the Welsh language and anti-oppressive practice.
1994   1 85644 291 8   134 pages

Perspectives on Discrimination and Social Work in Northern Ireland
Faith Gibson, Gill Michael and Dorothy Wilson
Training materials focusing on religious discrimination and its relevance to social work in Northern Ireland.
1994   1 85719 083 1   226 pages

Practising Equality
Julia Phillipson
A personal contribution on gender and anti-sexism in the context of the Diploma in Social Work.
1992   1 85719 001 7   76 pages

Disability Issues
Aims to help develop ideas about perceptions of disability and an understanding of anti-discriminatory practice related to disability in social work education and training.
1991   1 85719 000 9   28 pages   Also available on tape

For information on prices and availability, for a full list of CCETSW's publications, or to place an order please contact:

Mail Order Unit
CCETSW, Derbyshire House, St Chad's Street, London WC1H 8AD
Tel: 0171 278 2455   Fax: 0171 278 2934

Information Service
CCETSW, 78-80 George Street, Edinburgh EH2 3BU
Tel: 0131 220 0093   Fax: 0131 220 6717

Information Service
CCETSW, 6 Malone Road, Belfast BT9 5BN
Tel: 01232 665390   Fax: 01232 669469

Information Service
CCETSW, South Gate House, Wood Street, Cardiff CF1 1EW
Tel: 01222 226257   Fax: 01222 384764

RACEGENDERLANGUA
GEDISABILITYEQUALO
PPORTUNITIESSEXUAL
TYLAWGUIDANCEPRA
CTICERACEGENDERLA
NGUAGEDISABILITYEQ
UALOPPORTUNITIESSE
XUALITYLAWGUIDAN
CEPRACTICERACEGEN
DERLANGUAGEDISABI
LITYEQUALOPPORTUN

Index

References in this index are to paragraph numbers. The index should be used in conjunction with the contents page and, accordingly, references here are to subjects which might not easily be identified from the earlier list of contents.